BLEEDING BLUE

Giving My All for the Game

WENDEL CLARK

WITH JIM LANG

PUBLISHED BY SIMON & SCHUSTER

New York   London   Toronto   Sydney   New Delhi

Simon & Schuster Canada
A Division of Simon & Schuster, Inc.
166 King Street East, Suite 300
Toronto, Ontario   M5A 1J3

This Simon & Schuster Canada edition November 2016

SIMON & SCHUSTER CANADA and colophon are registered
trademarks of Simon & Schuster, Inc.

For information about special discounts for bulk purchases,
please contact Simon & Schuster Special Sales at 1-800-268-3216 or
CustomerService@simonandschuster.ca.

Clark, Wendel, 1966–, author
Bleeding blue : giving my all for the game / Wendel Clark.
Issued in print and electronic formats.
ISBN 978-1-5011-3598-9 (hardback).—ISBN 978-1-5011-4651-0 (html)
1. Clark, Wendel, 1966–. 2. Hockey players—Canada—Biography.
I. Title.
GV848.5.C557A3 2016 796.962092 C2016-902671-X
C2016-902672-8

Interior design by Lewelin Polanco

Manufactured in the United States of America

1 3 5 7 9 10 8 6 4 2

ISBN 978-1-5011-3598-9
ISBN 978-1-5011-4651-0 (ebook)

To my family; Kelvington, Saskatchewan;
and fans of the Toronto Maple Leafs.

Contents

BLEEDING BLUE

Introduction

On the morning of October 9, 1986, I was walking along Carlton Street towards Maple Leaf Gardens. It was a perfect fall morning in Toronto. It felt like a great day to play hockey. As I entered the Gardens, the noise of the street fell away, and the peace and quiet of the empty arena settled over me. I made my way to the dressing room, grabbed my sticks and a roll of tape, and then headed up into the empty stands for my usual game-day routine. I sat there looking out over the ice, slowly taping my stick and thinking through what that night would bring. I was trying hard to keep myself calm, but I had a lot on my mind. We were getting ready to face Patrick Roy and the Montreal Canadiens in the first game of my second pro season, and whenever we played Montreal, it was a special night. Toronto versus Montreal was as good as it got. It was always easy to get excited for those games, even more so when they were the home opener.

After the morning skate, I went home for some downtime and my typical pregame meal. I usually ate pasta and chicken. Over the course of an eighty-game season, though, that could get pretty repetitive, so sometimes I would change it up and have something like steak and potato—basically some starch and a piece of meat, and I was good to go. Back in 1986, I wasn't as concerned about having a perfect diet as today's players are.

After my meal, followed by a nap, I was ready to go. By four o'clock I was back at the rink, and my mind was already starting to get into game mode. The Habs were the defending Stanley Cup champions that year, and we all knew that if Patrick Roy was on his game that night, we'd have a tough time getting the puck past him.

In my mind, there was no better way to start the season than with a challenge like that. Not only was it an Original Six matchup in an iconic arena, but the energy in the building just before the game was incredible, as it always was. As is traditional for a Maple Leafs home opener, the 48th Highlanders marched out onto the ice to ring in the start of the new season in Toronto. The bagpipes and drums filled the arena, and as the music and noise from the fans rumbled through my chest, I couldn't wait to hit the ice. The crowd was rabid that night, as they were hoping we could beat the team that had just won the Cup. It must have been a big night, because a few of the boys even spotted John Candy sitting in the crowd. John was a big Leafs fan and went to a lot of our games.

We definitely fed off the energy at the Gardens that night, and we came out flying. Any Montreal fans there were disappointed as we won the game 7–4. Tom Fergus scored a hat trick, and the crowd was really rocking. In the third period, I scored a goal from the top of the circle, beating Roy to the far post. Roy got so pissed off after I scored that he threw his stick away. The boys were in a great mood in the dressing room after the game that night, and the whole city was energized. The next day, the story of our win over the Habs was on the front page of the *Toronto Star*.

Two nights later, the Buffalo Sabres were in town to face us in a Saturday-night matchup on *Hockey Night in Canada*. That morning, I hopped into my car and drove from my apartment on Madison Avenue down to Maple Leaf Gardens for our game-day skate. In my first year with the Leafs, I hadn't been old enough to sign for a lease on a car by myself, so my agent, Don Meehan, had rented me a grey four-door Plymouth Caravelle. Not exactly a hot car for a rookie. But in my second season, I had a sponsorship deal with a local dealership, so I cruised down Bloor Street that morning in a blue Oldsmobile Delta 88.

Because we'd played the night before, our skate that morning was pretty light, and afterwards I had time to make my way over to the bistro beside the Gardens for breakfast. The ladies there had the toast I liked—classic toasted Wonder Bread, with peanut butter— so it was my go-to breakfast stop. The ladies who ran the grill also would have soup and sandwiches for lunch, so it goes without saying that I was also in there a lot after practices.

After a few hours at home and another nap, it was back to the rink. It was a Saturday night, *Hockey Night in Canada*, and we would be facing the Buffalo Sabres. As I entered the Gardens, I could already feel the air in the place starting to buzz. We would need that energy, too—playing the Sabres was never easy for us. We tried everything to beat them, changing things up each time to try to find a setup that worked—taking the bus to Buffalo early, taking the bus there late, staying over in Buffalo, coming home right after the game—but it didn't matter what we did; Buffalo always seemed to have our number.

As I walked into the dressing room, I checked the board and saw that I would be playing with Russ Courtnall and Gary Leeman that night. They called us the "Hound Line" because all three of us, at one time or another, had played with the Notre Dame Hounds in Saskatchewan. Russ and I had actually played on the same midget team together in 1982, so every time we were on the ice together, we knew exactly what the other guy was doing and where he would be. Gary had been a couple of years ahead of us, but he was an incredible all-around athlete and his skills made us all better players.

I sat down at my locker, and before I did anything else, I picked up my classic red Titan TPM stick and started to tape it up for the evening's game. I was particular about what stick I used; my stick and my skates were my tools, my weapons, when I was on the ice, and to make sure I got the most out of them, I had to treat them just so. I started with the butt end, where I would do ten to fifteen wraps of the one-inch-thick tape. Then I taped the blade of the stick from heel to toe. I normally used black tape, but I felt like changing things up that night, so I chose white tape.

As far as getting my skates ready, that wasn't nearly as complicated. I didn't like sharp skates. I found that if they were too sharp or had too big a hollow between the edges of my skate blades, my legs would get tired from working too hard. The trainers knew that, so they knew to sharpen my skates only every two or three games. I would do a pregame skate, and if they felt good, I didn't sharpen them for the game. I figured there was no point messing around with a good thing.

As I walked down the hallway to the rink, I could hear the murmur of the crowd steadily build into a roar, and as I stepped out onto the ice, I could feel momentum from the previous game surging through me. We went through our warm-up, and everything was clicking. Our passes were on the tape, the puck was settling on our sticks, and our shots were on point. My legs felt good; in fact, the entire team seemed to have their legs that night. It was Saturday night, we were at the Gardens, and everything seemed to be going right. You can't ask for much more than that.

I lined up for the opening faceoff, and from the moment the puck hit the ice, I could feel it following me around all game. Some nights, I would have to work to get to the puck and I would find that it was bouncing away or just out of reach. But on my best nights—on that night—it was as though the puck was mine and mine alone. Instead of having to work for the puck, I made it work for me.

Early in the game, I scored my first goal of the night. We were on a five-on-three power play, and the Hound Line got down to business. After some work in the offensive zone, Russ feathered a pass to me through the crease, and I had all the time in the world to snap the puck home. Just three minutes later, Leeman set me up for my second goal of the evening. Leeman was an amazing athlete, and he did all the work. He fed me such an absolutely beautiful pass that, again, all I had to do was tap it in. We were flying, and we didn't show any signs of stopping, because only a minute after my second goal, Leeman and Courtnall set me up for my third goal of the night—I had a hat trick in the first period. But even though we'd scored a flurry of goals, the Sabres were hot on our heels. After the first period, the score was 3–3, and by the third period, Buffalo had taken a 5–4 lead. No matter how hard we battled, the Sabres kept coming right back at us. Then, midway through the third period, Leeman and Todd Gill made some nice plays as we broke out of our zone. I got the puck, and I suddenly found myself with some room in the neutral zone. I rushed across the Sabres' blue line, and Mike Ramsey, the Buffalo defenceman, went down on one knee to block my shot attempt. But I saw the move coming, so I waited a split second and then used Ramsey as a screen. By the time goalie Daren Puppa saw my wrist shot, it was too late to stop it. The game was tied 5–5 on my fourth goal of the game. After that, the offence dried up. Overtime solved nothing, and so the game ended in a 5–5 tie. (Yes, there were ties back then in the NHL.)

A tie is better than a loss, so we took our point and called it a night. As we walked back to the dressing room, I was still buzzing from my four goals. But I was also disappointed because we hadn't won the game. At the end of the day, that's all that matters, and every effort you make on a team is for that one thing. So when my absolute best didn't get us there, I wondered what I could or should have done differently.

After the game, we all headed out to Pat & Mario's, a restaurant over at Church and Front Streets. One of our rituals was that we would all go out as a team on Saturday nights, usually to Pat & Mario's, Brandy's, or Scotland Yard, a block south at Church and the Esplanade. In 1986, our downtown bar options were limited. Later, there was also Earls Tin Palace up at Yonge and Eglinton or Peter's Back Yard on King Street, and a few years later, the Phoenix and RPM opened up.

We never worried about going out on Saturday night as a team. We knew we had a practice the next day, but we were young and we could sweat it out. As we sat around with our beers, someone pointed out that I had five goals after the first two games of the season, which made me the league leader in goal scoring. We joked that I should enjoy it while it lasted.

I wish I'd taken that joke more seriously, because my time at the top of the league wouldn't last long. That night, as I sat there with my friends as a young man, I felt like I was on top of my world, with nothing but opportunity ahead of me. Nothing could stop me. Or so I thought. I would soon find out that there's one opponent you never see coming: yourself.

1

Growing Up in Kelvington

There's no loafing on the farm, so there's no loafing in a game."
As a kid, I heard those words from my dad a lot. When you grow up on a family farm like I did, you learn early on that everyone is expected to pull their weight on the home front.

Home for us was a grain and cattle farm that covered about a thousand acres when I was born, although we later expanded it to nine thousand acres. Our farm was in Kelvington, a tiny community of nine hundred people roughly 250 kilometres east of Saskatoon. You can't get much more small-town or rural than Kelvington, Saskatchewan. We had everything that any small rural town needs: a grain elevator, bank, post office, credit union, department store, hospital, retirement home, town hall, and, like in every small town in Saskatchewan, a Chinese restaurant. The one we had in Kelvington was called Ning's Café. In terms of things to do, the selection was a little more limited. We were big enough to have a motel and a hotel, although the motel was basically just a long strip of property just outside of town. The hotel was in town, and it had the one bar in Kelvington. There was also an auction market, a skating rink, a curling rink, and even a nine-hole golf course. The golf course was easy to find, as it was beside the water tower and the motel.

Golf in small-town Saskatchewan was different than what most people are used to. Our course had sand greens—oiled sand, to be exact. So, when you were on the green, you had to make a path in the sand just to putt your ball. I golfed on the course often as a kid, and my grandfather later brought the first golf cart to Kelvington. One of the most exciting moments I can remember was when Kelvington hosted the Saskatchewan sand greens golf championship. The tournament was held in different towns each year, and when Kelvington got its turn, believe me, it was a major deal and the whole community came out. That wasn't all that hard, of course. Because we were such a small town, everyone knew everyone in Kelvington; we all moved in the same circles. We only had one public school and one high school, so growing up, I knew every kid in the surrounding area.

My dad had been born in Kelvington in the middle of the Great Depression, and he spent his early life there. As a young man in the 1950s, he left town to play junior and minor pro hockey. He signed somewhere different every year, from Moose Jaw to Saskatoon to Philadelphia to Charlotte. Eventually, though, he headed back to Kelvington in his early twenties to work on the family farm. It was good timing, since my mom, who was from Springside, Saskatchewan—a town about 150 kilometres away that, if possible, was actually smaller than my hometown—had just moved to Kelvington to teach school. They met soon after Dad moved back, and it wasn't long before they were married and starting a family.

It isn't very hard to see where I got my work ethic. My parents, each in their own way, were the people most responsible for shaping me into the man I am today. But while my dad taught me a lot of the skills I would need to get to the NHL, it was my mom who showed me every day how important it is to get along with everyone and anyone around you.

Mom made sure we had three square meals a day. I'm talking about a hot breakfast, lunch, and dinner, day in and day out. Steak and potatoes (with plenty of bread and butter) was my favourite meal. Of course, growing up on a cattle farm, I had to like that. But it helped that my mom was also a heck of a cook—I would have eaten anything she put in front of me. I would often look in the fridge and complain that there was nothing to eat. She could look in the fridge, and the next thing you knew, there'd be three different meals sitting on the table. She would be mixing and matching things, and everything would be delicious. She really could cook up a storm.

But on a farm, nobody does just one thing. On top of taking care of all of us day to day, my mom was also the one who would run into town for spare parts if something on one of the farm implements broke. That allowed Dad and the hired men to keep working away on one of the many jobs that inevitably needed their attention. There's no question that the hardest-working person on our farm was my mom. She was the head chef, parts runner, and jane-of-all-trades.

We hired men during the seeding and harvest seasons—the busiest periods of the year for us—to get the jobs done in time. One constant was Tim Johnson. He was like family to us growing up. Tim was with us every year, helping out on the farm—he even lived in a little bunkhouse on our property. Tim was only ten years older than me. He had dropped out of school and started working for my dad at sixteen, which made him the cool guy in town because he had some money. As a young kid, I really liked Tim because he fixed all the things that we broke before my dad got home!

So, depending on what day of the year it was, my mom was cooking three meals for anywhere from five to fifteen people. And that doesn't even count the snacks we might be having at nine or ten o'clock in the evening when we had to work all night or the desserts that we got after most meals. You don't grow up on a farm without having good desserts, and they were my mom's specialty. The only bad dessert that she made was Christmas pudding; I hate Christmas pudding.

Growing up, I did the usual chores that any farm kid would do. On top of our grain farming, we also had a cow and calf operation. We had two hundred cows that we had to tend to every day. As kids, my brothers and I had to stand by the gates of the cow pen at feeding time and make sure none of them got out while my dad used the tractor to bring in bales of hay and feed for them. It would be minus-25 degrees Celsius outside, and we would be standing still, little kids guarding the entryway against the massive animals around us.

Come spring, our big job was tree planting. In Saskatchewan, you created your farmyards by planting trees to mark the border. My dad's philosophy was that by planting fresh trees every year, your yard would always be healthy. So, as the trees that my grandfather had planted fifty years earlier died off, we had to replace them with new saplings to keep the border from thinning out too much. We must have planted thousands of trees on our property over the years. We had two ways of getting the job done. Sometimes we would just dig a big hole and lay the tree in directly by hand. Other times we would put the trees into the ground using a potato planter. I or one of my brothers would sit on the back of the potato planter while the others towed it around with the tractor, and as the planter dug each hole, we'd drop the new tree into it. The days were long, but on a farm, even kids do whatever it takes to get the job done.

Harvest time was when things were busiest. On the farm, if it wasn't raining during the harvest, you would be working from 6 a.m. to 2 a.m. for two weeks in a row. The hired men would pray for rain just so they could have a break. The long hours weren't a choice, though. We had to work quickly to get the crops off the ground, because we never knew how long our window of good weather would last. So, as long as the weather held, we would stay out in the fields. The only thing that would stop us was the dew. The combine didn't work well if there was any moisture in the field, so dew on the crops meant the combine wouldn't thrash well. And even if the dew settled in, it didn't give us much of a break—we'd just have to work harder and faster once the crops were dry again.

At seeding time, the schedule was a little different, but the days were just as long. My dad used to get up at four in the morning and start seeding until the hired men arrived at six. At that point, Dad would go have a nap, and then he'd be right back out there, working alongside the others. Everyone got the same amount of sleep in the end, but it meant that more work got done throughout the day.

My days weren't all that different from those of other farm families. My brothers and I were the extra help the family needed to get the jobs done. It wasn't pretty or easy, but there were some perks. We all had parts of the farm that we liked best, but everyone knew my favourite thing was to go for a drive. As a young kid, I looked up to the guys who would drive all the machinery around the farm, and seeing them control those powerful machines made me want to do the same.

I drove a vehicle for the first time when I was six years old. We had one of those old Datsun pickup trucks with a five-speed stick shift, and it was the first car in which I could reach the pedals with my toes. Before I was ten, I was already driving small farm equipment. Once my dad saw that I was comfortable with the smaller vehicles, he decided to promote me to the bigger machines. One day, just after I'd turned ten, Dad told me that instead of coming home after school, I was to pick up our four-speed Ford tractor, which was being repaired at the John Deere dealership in town. It seemed easy enough—the machine was just a little bigger than our lawn tractor, and I'd driven that plenty of times. The dealership was right near my school in town, so to my dad, it made more sense for me to stop off there and bring the tractor home after school than it did for him to take time off work to head into town and pick it up.

I followed my dad's instructions, and after I got out of class, instead of catching the bus like I usually did, I walked to the dealership, grabbed the keys, and started driving the tractor home. My plan was to head through town and stop off at my grandma's house before continuing on home. I didn't realize that my route would take me right past the police station. As soon as I rolled by, one of the cops came flying out of the parking lot with the lights on. He made me pull over, and once he heard my story, he told me *he* would move the tractor. But when he got behind the wheel, the cop saw that there was more to the machine than he thought, and he realized he didn't have a clue how to drive it. My dad wasn't mad—it was his idea, after all. But he also refused to come pick me up. Work on the farm still came first. So I had to wait by the tractor with the cop until my mom came to collect me, the machine, and the ticket I'd been given for driving underage.

By the time I hit thirteen, I was consistently driving the bigger machines like the tractors, combines, and swathers. It didn't matter whether the engine had five horsepower or five hundred, I loved driving it. It's easier to experiment like that as a kid in a rural community. The population density in Kelvington is next to nothing. So when I was behind the wheel of a car, a five-hundred-horsepower tractor with double wheels in the front and the back, a grain truck, or anything else, I had nothing but space around me.

My parents never stopped me from driving. In fact, they encouraged it, because if I could drive, it meant I could work. We had that Ford tractor, along with a Datsun pickup and a smaller Toyota, and often, my mom might send me out to deliver meals to the crews in the field. She would finish the cooking and set it out, and when I got home from school, I'd hop in one of the little pickup trucks and take the food out to the guys. Especially at harvesttime, every minute was precious. We were all working from dawn until well after sunset, so we couldn't afford to have everyone walk back and forth from the fields to get their meals. Also, our farm was well spread out. It crossed lots of roads and was scattered around the town. It got to the point where parts of our land were up to twenty-four kilometres away from our house—you actually had to drive through town to get from one side of our property to the other. I'd leave school in the centre of town and walk home, then turn around and take the food to the crew, cruising along the numbered streets past the school, the post office, and the grain elevator with KELVINGTON stamped on the side. Everyone pitched in; we all knew that we had a role to play if we were going to get the job done.

• • •

I was the second of three sons in our family. My dad, Les, and my mom, Alma, had my older brother, Donn, in 1962. I was born in 1966, and then my younger brother, Kerry, came along in 1968.

You would think that three brothers growing up together on a farm would mean there were a lot of fights. But Donn, Kerry, and I never scrapped all that much. I never fought that much in school, either. I tried to never fight, because if my dad ever found out about me scrapping, my punishment at home would be way worse than anywhere else. My mom wasn't any more lenient. She had quit her job as a schoolteacher after I was born, but she still knew the other teachers and had plenty of that teacherly discipline to direct at us. If I did anything bad at school, she would have found out about it real quick. In a small town, you really can't get away with anything; if you do something bad in the morning, everybody knows about it by lunchtime. So I tried to stay out of trouble.

That being said, Donn, Kerry, and I still took up a lot of air. When I was growing up, everything happened outdoors. Our house wasn't big enough to play in, so we would get kicked out of the house a lot. And once we were outside, Mom wasn't letting us back in until it was time to eat. I can't blame her—it was a small farm home, too small for three boys to be running around in. Also, we weren't the only animals around. We always had family dogs—straight farm dogs that lived outside and were never allowed in the house, but when you added them to our mix, I'm amazed our mom didn't kick us off the property, let alone out of the house.

We had a basement, but it wasn't much more than a cold storage room and the furnace. If we were playing in there, we might as well have been outside. We preferred to be outdoors, anyway. Donn had his own room, but Kerry and I shared a bedroom, so for the two of us especially, being outside meant that there was more room for each of us.

We were also lucky that our closest neighbours were also our cousins. Neil, Darryl, and Rory were my cousins, and they were the same ages as me and my brothers. Of course, when I say they were our closest neighbours, they still lived half a kilometre down the road. Still, having them relatively close by was perfect for a sports-crazed kid like me. Whether we were playing three-on-three hockey, baseball, soccer, football, or any other team sport, the six of us could organize games right there without needing anyone else. To this day, I hate hearing the words "We have nothing to do." To an outsider, it might have seemed that Kelvington didn't offer much. But to the six of us, it was our entire world, and we couldn't have been happier.

Still, rural Saskatchewan isn't known for a whole heck of a lot. The scenery is beautiful, the people are kind, and the farming is nonstop. But one thing it *can* claim is cold weather. As a kid, I never gave the cold much thought or found it to be that bad. It was just a fact of life. I remember playing a hockey game when I was eight years old in Invermay, Saskatchewan. We were at an indoor rink, but even with a roof and four walls around us, it was minus-40 degrees on the ice. It was just too cold for us to sit on the bench between shifts. So the coaches and refs came up with a system where every player who wasn't on the ice went to the dressing room to keep warm. Every two minutes, the ref would blow his whistle, and both teams would change their lines. It worked for everyone . . . except the goalies. Those poor guys were on the ice the entire time.

As a young kid, I'd often play hockey wearing an unusual set of equipment. In the winter, it would get so cold that we couldn't wear regular hockey gloves. There wasn't enough insulation on them, so our hands would be frozen in no time. Instead, we wore regular winter mittens. On top of that, I would often wear a toque under my helmet, and I never went out without long underwear under my equipment. Sometimes even that wasn't enough, though, and I'd have to wear my regular pants and underwear under my equipment as well. It was as though I was dressed to go out and play in the snow, except I had all my hockey gear on, too. It was the only way we could play. And I always wanted to play.

My brothers and I spent a lot of time shooting the puck around in our yard. We didn't have an outdoor rink, but we had a goal at the end of our driveway, by the sidewalk, and that thing saw a lot of action. We placed three four-by-eight sheets of plywood behind the net to stop the puck if we missed. It was either that or we would be fishing pucks out of the snowbanks all night long. When it was too cold to stay outside, I would practise my shot inside the house. I would get down on my knees in the kitchen and use a ruler to shoot a marble against the bottom of the kitchen cabinets. Our kitchen had one of those old linoleum floors, so the marble really took off when I fired it. Those cabinets took a bit of a beating. And in the summers, we would even bring the net to our cottage so that we could keep playing all year round.

I shot so many pucks into that net over the years. I wouldn't ever call it practice, because I was having fun the whole time. As a kid, training and conditioning weren't a part of my life. Growing up on a farm, you don't need to go to a gym to get strong. Every chore on the farm was an exercise. We never saw it that way, of course. It was just the usual day-to-day stuff for us. But between the demanding work I did on the farm and all those evenings that I spent alone on the driveway, wristing puck after puck into the net, I was constantly training in one way or another.

I tried my hand at things other than sports. I played the saxophone in grades four through eight. I wasn't too bad, but slightly above average at best. When I was in grade eight, I was already missing a lot of school because I was travelling so much to play hockey. It got to the point that my music teacher told me I could keep taking lessons, but I couldn't play in the band if I was going to keep taking hockey trips at the same time. He said I had to make a choice. It was the easiest choice of my life. I said, "See you later, band."

My dad loved to see me out in the yard, shooting the puck, and he made sure I had sticks and pucks to play with. He used to buy sticks by the half dozen for me and my brothers. He would bring them home, and then he'd pull out a torch to heat up the blades and straighten them. He didn't believe in a curved stick, so when I learned how to play, it was with a stick that was as dead straight as Gretzky's. I wouldn't start using a curved blade until I got to junior.

There's a technique to a great shot, but it's also an art. I didn't have technology helping me—wooden sticks really didn't bend. For every shot I took on that driveway, with the light fading around me, I had to practise positioning my feet, controlling my hands, and shifting my weight. Everything had to be perfect if I was going to be able to shoot the puck hard.

My dad had all sorts of odd rules and directions for me when I was playing hockey. In my early years, I played defence, but my dad told me I wasn't allowed to ever slap the puck from the point. No slap shots, only wrist shots. I never found out why my dad insisted on that. Whenever I asked him why, he'd just say, "You're not going to slap the puck." Maybe it came from his time in the junior and pro ranks. It was like he had an idea of what real hockey should be like, and he wanted to make sure it was the way I played.

I did what he told me, though, and it didn't hurt me. Even though

I only took wrist shots in games, I was still scoring all the time. At one point, our team was winning by so much that our coach put a new rule in place: after a player scored three goals, he wasn't allowed to rush the puck past the offensive blue line. So if I was going to score, I had to shoot at the goalie from the far side of the blue line; I couldn't even skate into the other team's zone. While it made things a little harder, I still managed to find a way to score. That rule came into place when I was in that six-year-old league, and even back then, I could wrist the puck from the blue line and get it over the goalie's head. At six years old, none of the goalies were as tall as the net yet, so I was scoring on them bar down from outside the blue line.

When I was at another team's rink, I had parents chirping me all the time because of how I played. It never bothered me, though, because I was playing to win. My dad never said anything in response to the other parents—partly because he wasn't the kind of guy to react to noise like that, but also because he wasn't usually around to watch me play. My dad didn't regularly start watching me play hockey until I was playing junior in Saskatoon. He tried his best when I was younger, but the fact was that he was just too busy working. There was always something to do—harvesting crops, tending to cattle, or ploughing and seeding the land. He probably watched me and my brothers play baseball in the summer more than hockey in the winter, because our baseball games were on Sundays, his one day off. It also helped that my dad just loved baseball. He would come out, watch the ball tournaments from his lawn chair, and not have to worry about the farm for a few hours.

Mom ended up watching me more because she did most of the driving. Sometimes, after dropping me off, Mom would come into the rink to watch me play or practise. But other times, she would be in the car, taking a nap just so she could stay awake on the drive back to Kelvington.

My dad had a big influence on me when it came to the philosophy of hockey and my work ethic in general. His attitude was straightforward: if you played, you had to play hard. He would ask me, "If you're going to make the effort to get close to the net, why just shoot it? Make sure you shoot to score when you get there." My dad's view of hockey was similar to his view of work in general. If you're going to do something, do it right. And take pride in what you do. Good things don't just fall in your lap; you have to work for them, intensely and consistently, and if you're going to put the time in, you need to make the payoff worth the effort. On the farm, that meant long days and nights working to secure the best harvest, which would mean a better life for your family. And on the ice, it meant that if I ever got a chance to shoot the puck, I shot to score.

● ● ●

Everything in a small town in the winter revolves around the skating rink and the curling rink. If you needed to find someone, you went to the skating rink first and asked around. If they weren't there, you went to the curling rink. Usually, all the kids would be at the skating rink while the parents would be at the curling rink; parents usually hung out at the curling rink because it had a liquor licence, so they could get a beer there.

Although it was a small town, Kelvington had a good local hockey rink. It was my second home in a lot of ways. Although he'd quit his hockey career long before I was born, my dad had never left hockey behind. He ran a lot of the hockey programs in Kelvington—there was one for every age group. And Dad ran the rink in Kelvington before I was born—Barry Melrose's father, Jim, ran it when I was growing up. Years later, my dad was part of the group of men who got together to organize the new town arena. I remember driving the tractor inside the construction site, helping to level the ground for the new rink.

The town arena was home to one atom team, one peewee team, one bantam team, and one midget team. Once those four teams had practised, the ice was basically free for anyone who wanted to use it. It was a dream come true—nearly unlimited ice time only a few minutes from home. I made the most of it. Once I started skating, it was hard to get me to stop. I practised skills that my dad or coach had taught me, but I also took time to just play around. I would do anything to get more ice time, and sometimes I'd even end up in the arena all by myself. The guys who ran the rink were great. If there was a team about to go on after the rink had been flooded, I wasn't allowed to mess up the new ice with my skates. But they would let me go out with my boots on and stick in hand. Even like that, I could spend hours out there.

For me and my brothers, playing hockey beat watching it. The only games we watched were the big *Hockey Night in Canada* match-ups on Saturday nights at 6 p.m. I was perfectly happy about watching so little hockey. I didn't have hockey idols growing up the way my younger brother, Kerry, did, and I never dreamed of playing in the NHL. As a young kid in rural Saskatchewan, the NHL just seemed too far away. I was happy just to keep playing on my local rink whenever I had the chance.

But my parents could see that my skills were developing at a rapid rate, and they worked so hard to create opportunities for me. I was lucky, too, because my older brother, Donn, had paved the way for me. Donn was a tough defensive defenceman, and he had a lot of talent. He played Midget AAA for one year at Notre Dame. From there, he went on to play Tier II Junior A for the Yorkton Terriers, and then major junior for the Saskatoon Blades, until he broke his leg playing as an overager. I had watched the older guys in Kelvington develop around me and go on to play in other towns, but I never had any direct connection to them or their careers. Donn was the closest person to me who had left home to play hockey, and he planted the first seeds in my mind that I could have a hockey career.

It wasn't long before I was following in Donn's footsteps. When

I was eleven, I attended my first formal hockey camp. It was the Dennis Polonich Hockey School, and it was run by Dennis, who was playing for the Detroit Red Wings, along with a couple of future NHL stars, Brian Propp and Bernie Federko. I was on the ice with Polonich, Federko, Propp, and Barry Melrose, all of them awesome players who knew how to have fun with the game and teach skills to the kids. It was the first time I'd ever been introduced to anyone who actually played in the NHL, and I was amazed at their skill level. But more important, I learned how the game of hockey is about fun as much as it is a job. That's what I'd always felt, and I was amazed to hear that even the pros felt that way.

It wasn't long after that camp that I hit the next stage of my hockey career, and it was one that would test not only me, but my whole family. The Yorkton Bantam AAA team was holding tryouts. I was thirteen, and I needed better competition than what Kelvington could provide, so my parents and I decided I was ready to try to break into the higher ranks.

My older brother, Donn, was playing with the Yorkton Terriers at the time, and my dad asked me if I wanted to play rep hockey in Yorkton, too. I was ready for the challenge, but before he would let me try out, my dad wanted to make it clear he wasn't forcing me in any way, and that taking the next step was my choice. He had also decided he needed to be sure I was committed and actually wanted to play in Yorkton. So he laid it on the line for me. He said, "If you want to play in Yorkton, you phone the coach and ask for a tryout. I'm not doing it for you. If you want to go, I'll get you there. But I'm not *telling* you to go play there."

He was true to his word—my dad refused to phone the coach and set up the tryout for me. It was his way of finding out whether I really wanted to go or just had a passing interest. He wanted me to prove to him that I loved hockey, not that I merely liked it. It was a lesson that would stick with me. I realized that I would have to make choices for the right reasons, and I needed to stick with them and see them through. The message was clear: whether it's a body check, a wrist shot, a job, or a competition, you follow through.

I followed through on my end and called the Yorkton coach to ask for a tryout. A few weeks later, we made the two-hour drive south, and when we arrived, we found that there were eighty other kids there for the tryouts. I was considered an "out-of-towner," and it must have shown—I had never seen anything like it. Back in Kelvington, there were typically only twelve kids who "tried out" for the team, and naturally, we all made it. This would be the first time I would have to beat someone out to make a team.

When we got to the rink, there were two teams—one full of thirteen-year-olds and another of fourteen-year-olds. In small towns like Kelvington, the thirteen- and fourteen-year-olds still played together. But that year in Yorkton, they had enough kids trying out to fill two teams. Even though I was only thirteen, I tried out for the bantam team. I had no clue whether I was going to make it or not, but I think my dad knew. It was a test—the first of many—and I rose to the challenge. And my dad was right. Even though I was a year younger than most of the guys on the bantam team, I made the cut.

It was great hockey in Yorkton, and the competition at the AAA level was intense. But playing with older kids was nothing new to me. And it helped that the people on the team were so good to me. I made some great friends in Yorkton, and two of my cousins were teammates while I was there. One of them, David, was with me during my first year with the team, and then his brother, Dean, joined me the second year. David and Dean were cousins on my mom's side of the family, from Springside, Saskatchewan, and I didn't get to see them as much as my Kelvington relatives, so it was nice being able to play on the team and spend time with them.

For the two years that I played bantam rep hockey in Yorkton, I also played on Kelvington's bantam and midget teams. I played on three teams for two years, and on top of that, I also practised with the senior team in Kelvington. That was a lot of ice time, but it was an important stage in my development as a hockey player.

Sometimes, though, playing for so many teams would catch up with me. One night, I had to play games in Yorkton and Kelvington on the same evening. Yorkton's thirteen-year-old rep team was in Kelvington, playing in a tournament during the local winter carnival, and the Kelvington team wanted me to play for them. Barry Marianchuk, the coach of the Yorkton thirteen-year-olds, agreed that his team would wait for me to get back from Yorkton so that I could play with Kelvington, so as soon as I was done playing with the fourteen-year-olds in Yorkton, I raced out of the arena and hit the road. The Kelvington game was supposed to start at 8:30 p.m., but I didn't get there until about a quarter to nine. Nobody seemed to mind the delay—when the game started, the rink was still packed and the crowd was buzzing. The game was worth the trip, too. We beat the Yorkton team, 7–3, and I was lucky enough to score five goals. I don't think that poor goalie knew what hit him that night. As much as I liked scoring the goals, though, I liked winning the game even more. Especially because it meant so much for my hometown.

Playing at the AAA level in Yorkton could be tough at times. The real challenge was just getting to the rink in time for practices and games. Kelvington was 150 kilometres from Yorkton, and we drove the two hours back and forth for every single practice and game. That was no small feat. And because communities in Saskatchewan are so spread out and the population density is so low, we had to drive long distances for road games against other AAA teams. We might have a Friday night game all the way out in Swift Current, which meant a five-hour drive to the game and a five-hour drive home after. It took a lot of dedication to play hockey at that level in rural Saskatchewan.

My mom did most of the driving. I had to leave school at 2 p.m. just to be able to get to Yorkton in time for a practice at five o'clock. We would get home at 2 a.m., and then I'd pass out until I had to catch the school bus at seven thirty the next morning. But I wanted to play at that higher level, so I was willing to do whatever it took—I didn't think of it as a chore. My mom was the one making the big sacrifice. The time investment was one thing, but my mom gave up so much more than that to help me. She had my brothers to think about, and the farm constantly on her mind. And driving in Saskatchewan in the winter is far from stress-free. We never left the house without a survival kit packed in the trunk of the car: candles, a blanket, snow boots, a snowsuit, and a lighter. Because if our car ever broke down in the middle of the highway on a winter night somewhere between home and Prince Albert or Moose Jaw, there was a real chance we wouldn't make it if we were unprepared. That's life in the winter in Saskatchewan.

Considering how much effort it took from my parents just to get me to games, I kept my dad's lessons in mind and made my effort count when I got there. Our games were a full sixty minutes—no family wanted to drive halfway across the province for a twenty-five- or thirty-minute game. In my first year with the Yorkton Terriers, I started to figure out new strategies to make myself most effective in a game. I played my first year of bantam hockey with no face mask. After that first year, though, the rules dictated that we had to wear a half shield that covered the top half of our face. But that half shield wasn't the kind of Plexiglas visor you see today; it was a wire cage. It looked a lot like a lacrosse mask. It was designed to protect your eyes, but I discovered that you could still fit the blade of your stick between the spaces on the cage.

So, when we went from helmet only to face masks, I came up with a new tactic. If a guy was coming at me on a one-on-one, I would punch him in the face. Not hard enough to knock him down or hurt him; just hard enough to throw him off or rattle him and let me take the puck. All athletes will bend the rules to whatever works in order to win. It has nothing to do with what's fair and what's not fair—you're just playing to win.

Because the teams playing each other were so far apart, there were very few people in the stands for most of my games with York-ton. The parents of the guys on the home team might come out, but the only ones there for the visiting team would be whoever drove in the car pool or rode in the bus. That was normal to me—having played most of my hockey in Kelvington, I never expected to see massive crowds at a game. In just over a year, though, that would change drastically.

2

Hitting the Road

Given the amount of hockey I was playing and the level I was at, my parents knew that the pace I was going at wasn't about to slow down. They realized that they wouldn't be able to keep up with all the travel it took to get me to my games, while also running the farm. So, when I was fifteen years old, we decided I would have to go away for school. Luckily, we knew just where to look: Wilcox, Saskatchewan.

Wilcox isn't known for much—the town effectively came into being when eight settlers tossed their bags out of a train and pitched their tents by the side of the tracks in the early twentieth century. But the one thing that Wilcox does have to brag about is its hockey team, the Notre Dame Hounds.

My older brother, Donn, had gone to Notre Dame as a sixteen-year-old and played on their Midget AAA team. So my family knew what the school, the hockey, and the academics were all about. I wanted a challenge, and we recognized that Notre Dame would be the best place possible for me to play. And my parents also knew that, if I was living at Notre Dame, I would actually go to school. If you're housed with a billet in a bigger city, there isn't quite the same pressure to go to classes each day. In Wilcox, there wasn't much to do *but* go to school and play sports.

First things first, of course: I'd have to make the team. The odds weren't exactly great: there were two hundred kids trying out for the school's various teams that year. When I arrived for the tryouts, the coaches were dividing kids into various groups based on their age and skill, and I had no idea which of those teams I would be a part of or what any of them meant. Was one level for the kids who were definitely going to make it? Would I want to be moved to another, more competitive group, or stay in the one I was assigned? And to make things even more difficult, the Midget AAA team was usually made up of sixteen-year-olds, but I was only fifteen at the time, so I knew it was going to be an uphill battle to make that lineup.

The Hounds were legendary in minor hockey; those who did make the cut often went on to have lasting careers in hockey. Russ Courtnall and Mitch Messier were both Hounds players at one point. The team in the year ahead of me was especially loaded with talent. They had Gary Leeman, Gord Kluzak, James Patrick, and Brian Curran. The latter three were defenceman, and all of them were over six feet tall—on a midget-age team! You could make the argument that that team was the greatest midget team ever assembled. They were that good.

On top of that, it turns out my family had some personal history with Notre Dame. When my dad played junior hockey in the early 1950s, he served a long suspension after an unusual incident—he went after the goal judge. This was in the old days, when there was no glass behind the net, only a mesh fence, and as my dad went after the judge, all the fencing came down on top of the poor guy. We found out years later that the founding father of Notre Dame, Père

Athol Murray, was actually the commissioner of the league when my dad was suspended. Père Murray wasn't at Notre Dame when I went to school—he had passed away in 1975—but if my dad had recognized that connection, I'm not sure he would have sent me to Notre Dame.

The tryouts were tough. A lot of the guys were older and bigger than me, so I had to really push it to hold my own against them. Round after round of cuts was made, and it was both a relief and a thrill every time I saw that I would get to keep playing. It wasn't until the very last cuts were made that I found out I was one of five underagers (fifteen-year-olds) who had made the school's top team.

Those of us who made it were so excited to be on the team that year. A roster spot with the Hounds meant more games, more competition, and more intensity. And for a lot of guys, it meant taking one step closer to the ultimate dream of playing in the NHL. But the hard part was still to come.

• • •

My first year in Wilcox was the first time I'd lived away from home, and the first month was a bit of a shock. I remember walking into my dorm for the first time and seeing just how many people I'd be living in close quarters with—we lived four to a room. It was a big adjustment to make. It helped that we were all on the same page, though. All the students came from out of town, and everyone was there because they loved and excelled at sports, so we had a fair bit in common.

In my first year, my roommates were Pat Elynuik, who was also from Saskatchewan, Vince McMillan, and William Soo. William was from China, and he barely spoke a word of English; he'd been sent to Notre Dame so that he could practise speaking it. William was really smart, and he picked up on the rhythm of the school really quickly. He got up every morning at four o'clock and had a hot shower before getting back into bed for a few more hours of sleep. The first times he did it, I couldn't understand what he was doing. But I quickly realized that there was only hot water for about ten minutes every morning. As four hundred people got up and went to the showers and sinks at the same time, it quickly ran out. Most people found themselves rushed or stepping into a jet of frigid water. Not William Soo, though. He woke up feeling fresh as a daisy because he was smart enough to get up before everyone else and have a hot shower every day. I didn't have many problems with the showers, but that's because I had my own system. I discovered that, as long as I made it to class in the morning, it didn't matter whether or not I made it to breakfast. That was my cue to sleep in as long as possible most days.

I wasn't missing too much by skipping breakfast. The food at Notre Dame wasn't as good as my mom's. It was basic, old-time grub. But then again, those great ladies at Notre Dame had to cook for more than four hundred people every day—it was like running an army mess hall. Cheese sandwiches were a staple in my years at Notre Dame. Most guys supplemented the school food with care packages from home that got delivered to their dorm rooms all the time. But even then, nothing was guaranteed. If an "old boy" came around, he might help himself to the care packages sent to the "new boys." "Hey," he might say, "what are *we* eating tonight?"

I grew up a lot that first year at Notre Dame. I understood very quickly that I would have to solve my own problems—all the typical stuff that kids go through while growing up. You're in grade nine and someone in grade twelve wants to beat you up? Mom and Dad aren't stepping in, so you'd better step up.

Sometimes, you had to take a stand for serious issues. Other times, it was just bragging rights that were on the line. The dorms were full of boys and young men from fourteen to eighteen years old, and every now and then, we would have these epic, all-out pillow fights that pitted the dorms against each other. I was in the Gunner dorm, which was about one-third the size of the other two—Chopper and Badger—so we had our work cut out for us. Guys took these fights seriously. The football players on campus would put on their full gear for them, and some kids would make specialty pillows to fight with—some of them even put books inside their pillow cases, just to gain an edge. The fights eventually got so far out of control that some kids had to got to the hospital—it can really happen when you're being beaten up by ten or twelve guys, all armed with pillows—and the school eventually banned them outright.

As soon as a fight started, I knew to never stop swinging. I recognized that if I was doing most of the hitting, I would never get hit too badly in return. The key was to keep my arms moving at all times. A good feather pillow, bunched up solidly at the end, could deal a solid hit. Russ Courtnall was at Notre Dame at the same time as me, and he swears he watched me knock down twenty guys in a row in the hallway with my pillow.

Slowly and surely, I started to find my place. Notre Dame seemed to be made for me. I was surrounded by guys my age, and we were all connected by a love of sports. You could rely on the fact that there would be some kind of game going on twenty-four-seven. It might have been one that my buddies and I had made up in the dorm. Or it might have been a practice with the Midget AAA team. Or just a pickup game of soccer happening on the field outside the dorms.

Still, living in a situation like that can be challenging. You're all young men, and you're completely enveloped in a high-stakes, competitive environment. You live in a bit of a bubble, and you're all tossed into it without much preparation, so everyone is learning as they go. There are kids from different walks of life—different athletes from different backgrounds—and you have to find some common ground. Sports was our shared language. It let us move beyond our individual teams and get to know a broader group. Guys on the hockey team might find a best friend from the rugby squad or football team. The fact that we all just lived and breathed sports and would do anything to keep playing the games we loved let us connect and get over the awkward or difficult challenges that living together might bring.

That love for sports was one of the most important things I learned at Notre Dame. To make it in hockey, you have to love it. If two guys show equal talent, the guy who loves it will beat the one who only likes it. That's true in life, really, no matter what the job. And at Notre Dame, with two hundred kids trying out, you had to love it to make—and stay on—the team. Fortunately, we had some excellent coaches to make us better players.

When you're an athlete between fifteen and seventeen, you're like putty waiting to be shaped, and if you get the right coach at that time, it can make a huge difference in your development. Barry MacKenzie was the coach for the AAA team in my first year at Notre Dame, and then Terry O'Malley would become the coach in my second year. Barry and Terry were the best two coaches I could have ever asked for. They made everybody better players, and they were great for our age group. Both coaches taught the game as well as anyone I had ever been with. They did it in very different ways, but each man got his message across.

Barry was not only our coach for my first year at Notre Dame, but he was also a teacher and the principal at the school. Barry was a no-nonsense kind of guy, just as he was when he played for Canada at the 1968 Olympics. His manner was very straightforward, and his mindset was "This is how you play, and it's how you *have* to play." There was no debating or negotiating your role on the team with Barry.

Terry was more soft-spoken, as fluid with his words as he was a skater. Terry was a smart guy—he was similar to Nick Lidstrom in how he saw the game, angles, and positions. But more than just being able to see those things on the ice, he was also a great teacher, and he could break down all the little things for us to show us how to be better players. Terry played in the Lake Placid Olympics in 1980 as a forty-year-old, so I knew that if I could play the way he taught, I would be much better for it.

That first year under Barry MacKenzie, we all worked insanely hard. And it paid off. In my first year with the Hounds, we went all the way to the 1982 Air Canada Cup—now known as the Telus Cup—which was the national midget hockey championship in Canada, bringing together the top teams from each province. The tournament was in Victoria, British Columbia, that year, and we had a great round-robin, dropping only one game out of five. But when we got to the quarterfinals, we lost a close game to the Cape Breton Colonels, who would go on to take the bronze medal that year.

Losing in any playoff is disappointing, but we still had a lot of potential. The next year, 1982–83, we set our sights on getting back to the Air Canada Cup. But to do that, we would have to go through the Regina Pat Canadians in the Saskatchewan finals. Regina was our major rival that year and was loaded with talent, with guys like Brent Fedyk and Selmar Odelein—both future NHLers—on the team. Their skill was just too much for us, and Regina won the provincial championship before going on to win the Air Canada Cup, too. We got a measure of revenge, though. After the provincial finals that year, we played in a big western Canadian tournament that used to be held in Swift Current called the Tournament of Champions. That time, we got the better of Regina's team in the finals. It wasn't the same as the Air Canada Cup, but it was something. Every midget tournament out west was huge. Not only were the stands full of scouts at those tournaments, but the kids playing would be signing autographs, even though they were only fifteen or sixteen years old. That's just how big a deal those tournaments were.

Getting a taste of play at the national level made me hungry for more. I loved playing with the Hounds, and I wanted to win with them. We made such a great run with them my first year, and I was even more fortunate to have had a second chance with them, considering that I wasn't even supposed to be at Notre Dame for a second season.

• • •

When I was playing bantam in Yorkton, there was no Western Hockey League draft. Instead, each team submitted a list of players it wanted to claim the rights to. I had been listed on the Regina Pats' player list, meaning that the major junior team considered me one of its prospects and no other team could sign me. But if you were fourteen or under and a team put you on their player list, your name counted as two spots. It was a risk-reward system. If a team believed in you enough, they'd sacrifice a roster spot to land you at a young age. The Pats had done that, but they eventually decided they didn't want use up the extra roster spot to keep me—they didn't think I was big enough.

After Regina took me off their list, the Saskatoon Blades put me on theirs, and during my first season with the Notre Dame Hounds, I found out that I had made the Blades team for the 1982–83 season. I was loving my time at Notre Dame, but after I found out about the Blades, I focused on moving up to the next level.

At the start of what would have been my second year with the Notre Dame Hounds, I attended the Saskatoon Blades training camp. I made the team out of camp, and I thought that I was on my way to playing in the Western Hockey League. I moved in with my billets in Saskatoon, I enrolled in school, and I started training with the team. But then I found out my dad had other ideas. I was at my billets' house one night when there was a knock at the door around midnight. We were shocked to open the door and find my mom standing on the porch. She told me to pack my bags because she was taking me back to Notre Dame.

I couldn't believe it. Needless to say, the three-hour drive back to Notre Dame wasn't fun. As we drove, my mom told me how my dad had been out on the combine when he called her on the radio, saying, "Go pick up Wendel. He's going back to play midget." Sitting in the car with my mom, I barely said a word. Inside my head, I swore, shouted, and raged. But out of respect to my parents, I said nothing. I just sat there and watched the world go by as we left Saskatoon and headed back to Wilcox. There was no way I was going to vent my frustration on my mom just because I was upset. If I did, I knew my dad would find out, and that's when the trouble would really start.

My mom dropped me off in Wilcox, and instead of being happy to see familiar surroundings, I was fuming. It took months for me to finally get over the move. It was late November when Daryl Lubiniecki, the general manager of the Saskatoon Blades, reached out to me at Notre Dame and told me to call home and sort things out with my parents. He assured me that the Blades weren't turning me away and that he and the team weren't upset that I had returned to Wilcox. Saskatoon had a good junior team that year, they didn't need me to win, and the team wanted me to develop more at Notre Dame before joining the Blades the next year.

We had no cell phones, so we didn't talk to our parents every day. At Notre Dame, you could make one weekly call from the pay phone at the end of the hallway, and that was it. There was only one phone for the entire floor of the dorm—two hundred kids. And unless you were lucky enough to have a calling card, you had to call collect. If your parents didn't pick up or accept the charges, you were out of luck.

That year, my older brother, Donn, was an overager on the Blades, so my parents had some experience with what the play in the WHL was like. It was fast and rough, and everyone was out to make a name for himself in any way possible. That year in Saskatoon, there were at least three bench-clearing brawls. And that's just counting their games against the Regina Pats! My parents knew that I played a physical game, and they figured that, as a sixteen-year-old, I didn't need to be getting hammered by twenty-year-olds on a nightly basis—which wasn't a possibility, it was an inevitability. I didn't start really growing and filling out until I hit sixteen. Height-wise, I was fine, but I needed to match that height with some mass. My parents thought an extra year of midget-level hockey would help me mature and develop so that I could enter the junior ranks a little stronger, a little faster, and a little smarter.

In retrospect, it was the right decision. That second year of Midget AAA was incredibly useful for me. I played on the power play and killed penalties, logged a lot of minutes, and honed my shot, which helped me score twenty-one goals in only twenty-seven games. I had a chance to refine every aspect of my game in ways that wouldn't have happened if I'd been in Saskatoon.

That year at Notre Dame also taught me the importance of home-ice advantage. Our home rink was in a retrofitted barn, and in the dead of winter, it could easily be minus-25 in there. Nothing on you would ever warm up, and icicles would be hanging off the face mask on your helmet. It was so cold in our rink that, when city kids would come in to play us, they would be shocked because they had never been in a rink that cold before. They would look around with expressions that said, "What are we doing in this old barn?" The cold would slowly eat away at them and sap their energy throughout the game—most of the time, they couldn't wait for the game to end just so they could get on the bus and get back home. But we were used to it, and we loved the edge it gave us.

But when my second season with the Hounds was up and we'd returned from beating Regina at the Tournament of Champions, midget hockey was over. It was time for the next step in my hockey career. Notre Dame had given me so much, but there was nothing more I could learn there. I could have stayed, played on the school team, and then gone to college, like Mitch Messier did. But I decided to take a different path. A new challenge was waiting for me. It was time for me to make my entrance into major junior hockey.

• • •

While Saskatoon isn't huge—the population was about 180,000—for me, coming from Kelvington, it was more than big enough. And after the previous season's false start, I was excited to get back and really make the city and the team my new home. In my mind, I had waited long enough to take this step, so I wanted to make an immediate impact.

At about the same time I was making the move to the Blades, I was being scouted by some U.S. colleges. Technically, I can say that I was offered early acceptance to Yale—I received a college offer from them when I was only sixteen. It might not have been an academic scholarship, but at least I could have said I had gone to an Ivy League school! But I didn't get too far down that path. By this point, I had my eyes set on playing for the Saskatoon Blades.

When I made the jump to junior hockey with the Blades, both they and the Regina Pats had their games broadcast on the radio. The teams had a huge rivalry, playing each other fourteen times a year—two exhibition games and twelve regular-season games. Then Prince Albert got a team in the WHL, and we had another major provincial rival. Games with those teams that weren't emotional, hyped-up showdowns were rare.

It was easy to get caught up in the whirlwind and lose sight of everything other than hockey. Luckily, I had the right people around me, and that helped keep me grounded. I had an outstanding billet family to live with when I played in Saskatoon. My teammate Curtis Chamberlin and I lived with Ray and Nettie Fenner during our first year with the Blades. Curtis and I were in the same grade, so it made sense that we'd live with the same billet family. While living in Saskatoon, I went to Walter Murray Collegiate, and then I joined a number of other local boys on the Blades at Marion M. Graham Collegiate.

Ray and Nettie were amazing people—they were an extension of my parents. And, my parents were pleased to find out, the Fenners were very strict. When you're the billet family for a bunch of sixteen- to eighteen-year-old hockey players, you *need* to be. Especially if there's more than one player in the house. The Fenners didn't let us get away with anything, and they wouldn't do things that other billet families might do, like give us a credit card or let us stay out all night. If they set a curfew, you had to be home on time—end of story. It was their home and we had to live by their rules.

But Ray and Nettie were also incredibly warm people, and they took great care of me. I had awesome food, three square meals a day. (Good thing, too—playing in the WHL back then, I was making forty-eight dollars every two weeks. It paid for my gas in my truck, but not much else.) And they were passionate hockey fans, too. They were at all the games, and Ray, who worked as a heavy-equipment mechanic, servicing buses and trucks and large vehicles and machinery, was a regular rec league player.

From the very beginning, the Blades felt like a step up from the Hounds. In my first year, there were hockey cards of us, sponsored by the Saskatoon Police. And Shell Oil printed up full-page hockey posters that would be inserted into our game programs. At each home game, the program would have an insert of a different player, with a space at the bottom for our signatures, which we would fill in during team-sponsored autograph sessions. I couldn't wait to see myself featured on the insert. But when I finally got my hands on one of the programs, someone pointed out a problem: the printer had spelled my name wrong. There I was, wearing a big smile and my Cooperall pants, and my last name was spelled with an *e* at the end—Clarke. I couldn't believe it. I had seen my first name, Wendel, spelled wrong all the time, but I'd never seen someone spell *Clark* wrong before. Apparently, *Clarke* was the Catholic spelling, but I wasn't Catholic. Then it sank in: it was the 1980s, and the biggest Clark back then was Bobby Clarke, the pride of Flin Flon, Manitoba, a hockey legend so famous that he even influenced the makers of youth hockey cards. When I realized that, I just shrugged and said, "I haven't made it yet, so of course they can't spell my name right!"

Although I enjoyed Saskatoon, life with the Blades meant I spent a lot of time away from town. My first year of junior was also my introduction to the infamous bus trips that came with life in the Western Hockey League. Our longest bus trips would take us to Victoria—a twenty-six-hour drive for one game. On some of our road trips we'd drive even farther, starting off in Kelowna and Kamloops, then heading down to Victoria, Seattle, and Portland. We would drive down there, play six games in seven days, and then come straight back home to Saskatoon.

Despite all the travel, I only missed six days of school that year. On a typical weekend, I would play Friday, Saturday, and Sunday, anywhere from Victoria to Calgary to Medicine Hat to Lethbridge. After the Sunday game, I might not get back until five in the morning. By 7:30 a.m., I'd be awake again and then off to pick up some breakfast on my way to school. I can't say how alert I was in class, but at least I was there.

Looking back, I should have spent more time in school when I was in Saskatoon, because technically, I had more time on my hands. On the surface, it looked like I was tight for time—up early in the morning, playing hockey once or twice a day, and then school, and before I knew it, the day was done. But even with all that, really, I was finished by four o'clock most days. I could have been managing my time better and applying myself more. On the bus, there were no movies, no computers, and no MP3s—at that point, Sony Walkmans had just arrived. So there wasn't a lot to distract us on those bus trips. I should have been using that time to study.

Two of the guys I played with in Saskatoon found the time. Larry Korchinski, who won an award as a student athlete, is a lawyer now.

And Greg Holtby—whose son Braden plays goal for the Washington Capitals—took first- and second-year university courses while playing junior. If those guys could take university courses, I should have been able to take my high school homework with me and get it done.

There were parts of school I really liked. I enjoyed math and algebra in particular, probably because they came more easily to me than other subjects. But instead of studying on the bus, I preferred to sit right by the stairs at the front and watch the road, because I love driving and talking with the bussie. The bus drivers liked it because it meant they had someone to talk to on the long, dull drives. The drivers would sleep during our games so that they could drive all night to our next city. The least I could do was keep them entertained as they drove. And those drivers could make their way through anything—brutal weather, bad roads, and mountains. It was inspiring to watch how calmly they dealt with whatever was being thrown at them. With so many people depending on them, they had to be perfectly cool and in control.

Early in my first year with the Blades, I decided to drive out to Humboldt, about one hour from Saskatoon, where my brother Donn was coaching the local team. I had some buddies—Kelly Chase and Neil Clark—who were playing for him, and so Curtis and I decided we'd drive out to watch the game and then hang out with the guys after the game.

Well, things didn't go exactly as we planned. As we were driving back to Saskatoon, we got caught in the middle of a blizzard. The snow was coming down in sheets, and we were following the tracks of another car that was just ahead of us. Wrong call. We were driving in its tracks when, all of a sudden, we realized that the car ahead of us had gone into the ditch alongside the road, and we'd followed it right in! So there we were, halfway between Saskatoon and Humboldt at midnight in the freezing cold. Of course, being teenagers, we hadn't dressed for the weather, and we didn't have cell phones. So we did the only thing we could—we flagged down the first lift we could find headed in either direction. Of course, the first person to drive by was driving back to Humboldt, so we found ourselves headed back there for the night. When we finally got there, we had to phone Daryl Lubiniecki, the coach and GM of the Blades, to tell him we wouldn't be at practice the next morning. I told him we were in Humboldt and explained what had happened to my truck in the blizzard. He wasn't too impressed. But we made it through, and really, it's the setbacks we face that make us who we are.

That night, I was at the mercy of the weather and luck. I promised myself I'd be prepared from then on and wouldn't let something like that happen again—I wanted to control my own fate. But I was young, and I still had some learning to do on that front.

● ● ●

There was no fighting for me until I started playing junior. I wasn't the kind of guy who got into scraps off the rink, and I had absolutely no fights in my minor hockey career. I wasn't even close to having one until I started playing with the Saskatoon Blades, one night early in my first season there. We were playing the Lethbridge Broncos in a chippy game. Things got so heated that, late in the third period, we were short of defencemen on the bench—so many of them were either in the penalty box or had been thrown out of the game. Looking around, Daryl told us we had to keep ourselves in check—we couldn't afford to have any more guys kicked out of the game.

Given how intense the game had been, I wanted us to walk away with the win. That would make all the suffering worth it. So I took Daryl's words to heart, and I tried to keep a cool head. But as time was winding down, the Broncos took one more run at us, and they sent J. C. McEwan after me. I saw J. C. coming, and my first instinct was to drop my gloves and meet him head-on. But I remembered Daryl's orders—don't fight, and don't risk getting kicked out of the game. So when J. C. got to me, I dropped to the ice and covered up.

As I turtled in front of the three thousand fans in the arena, I felt absolutely horrible. I lay there and took J. C.'s punches until Joey Kocur, one of my teammates on the Blades, came over and took him on to get him off my back. For as long as I could remember, I'd known Joey was tough. We grew up playing together on the same teams in Kelvington, and even when he was as young as five years old, everyone could see that. In junior, Joey had a six-foot body and a big man's mentality to go along with it. People would look at Joey's baby face and see him smiling as he fought, and they wouldn't take him seriously. But I don't know if there's anybody who had a harder one-punch than Joey. Joey was a skilled player as a kid. But when he got to junior, he realized that he wasn't as skilled as a lot of other guys, so he decided that his ticket to a spot on the team was to fight. By his last year in Saskatoon, Joey had acquired a reputation as the toughest guy in the WHL by far. That gave him a lot of space to work with, and he scored forty goals and forty-one assists. Joey was tough, but he could also play the game. He was a prime example of a player who earned presence on the ice with his toughness, and having him as a teammate made you feel safe.

I was grateful to Joey for helping me out, but I didn't like the fact that someone had to come to my defence. After the game, I kept reliving the moment when I'd fallen to the ice instead of standing my ground. All the ways I tried to justify it—I was just following the coach's instructions, it was good that I didn't take a penalty—sounded like poor excuses. I promised myself I would never let that happen again as long as I played. I vowed that I would do all my own fighting from then on; I wanted to lead and fight for the guys around me, not hide and make them feel like I expected them to fight my battles.

So the next time we played Lethbridge, I dropped my gloves the very first time I ran into J. C. on the ice. I knew J. C. was a good fighter—he had had a few good bouts with Joey, and if someone was taking on Joey, they knew what they were doing. It was my first fight, but I held my own, and it was over before I knew it. Afterward, my teammate Dan Leier told me he had no idea I could fight the way I did, especially against an experienced enforcer like J. C.

After that, I started to get into more and more fights. I went from never fighting in minor hockey to dropping the gloves at least thirty times in each of my junior seasons. My next two fights after J. C. were against Al Conroy and then Bob Rouse—Al was a particularly feisty forward, and he and I fought twice in the same game. The more I fought, the more I found I was having fun doing it. Nobody has to force you to fight when you enjoy doing it. I didn't study technique or develop a strategy, either; there was never any science behind what I was doing. I preferred to throw rights, but my fight plan was simple: strictly offence, with whatever hand was free. There was a learning curve, for sure. I broke my nose only once in my hockey career, and it was during that year in junior. And I pretty much played my whole first year in Saskatoon with black eyes. But over time, my face and body got so used to the physical punishment of the fights that they didn't bruise as much.

Still, I didn't want to be known as just a fighter; I wanted to be a well-rounded defenceman. And I had the right talent around me to help me become a better player. Dave Chartier was my defence partner and our team captain during my first year in Saskatoon. Even though we were partners on defence, Dave still introduced himself at the start of every game as though we had never met. He told me he did that because he never saw me the rest of the game—I would have the puck in the offensive zone the whole time, while he stayed home on defence.

My failed fight against J. C. taught me that skill alone wouldn't be enough to carry me through a game. I needed an edge to my game, something that would let me channel my competitiveness into success, whether that meant scoring a goal or landing a punch.

It was then that I realized that the best player who's all hands has to play like a fourth-line player who's all heart. A lot of times, skilled players don't need to play that way, because they can let their ability carry them along. But that fourth-line guy has to throw everything he has into every second, or he can't play. I wanted to have the best of both worlds, because that's how you make superstars. When you get a guy who is talented but also loves what he's doing, then you have something special.

As time went on, I saw the proof of that. I played with Dwaine Hutton in Saskatoon, just before he was drafted by Washington in the NHL. Dwaine joined the Blades halfway through my first year in Saskatoon, and he put up forty-three points in only thirty-five games. But it seemed to me that he was also a guy who only liked the game, rather than loved it. He was so good. The best skater you would ever see, a total phenom. In that sixteen-and-under age group, Dwaine was easily one of the best players I ever skated with. And then, all of a sudden, he was done. I bumped into him about ten years later in Calgary, and he told me, "I messed up." I give him credit, because he was man enough to admit that it was his poor on-ice attitude that had ended his hockey career.

The flip side to Dwaine Hutton was Kelly Chase. Kelly was a real tough guy from Porcupine Plain. He and I met when Donn coached him in Tier II in Humboldt. We were fifteen and started hanging out. It wasn't long until we were best friends, and we've stayed that way ever since. After he played in Humboldt, Kelly went to a tryout in Moose Jaw and got cut. Then he went to a tryout in Saskatoon and made it. The year that I left to play in the NHL, Kelly joined the Saskatoon Blades.

It was my dad who helped Kelly get that tryout in Saskatoon. Dad phoned Daryl Lubiniecki and asked him to give Kelly a shot. He told Daryl, "Kelly is a good team guy. He'll do anything you ask." Kelly ended up making the Blades and became a key player. He never stopped working, he persevered, and he played in the minors and carved out a nice NHL career for himself. That's loving the game and never quitting. It doesn't matter where you're from: if you truly love what you do and are willing to do anything to play, you will make it.

There were a lot of guys I came across in junior who had that same approach and who went on to have long careers. In my first year in Saskatoon, Ray Ferraro—he's a hockey analyst for TSN now—scored 108 goals and had 192 points with the Brandon Wheat Kings, all in a single season. The Wheat Kings also had a defenceman named Cam Plante, who had 140 points that same year. Between Ray and Cam, we knew that we had to score a lot of goals anytime we played Brandon, because those two were bound to score at least two or three of their own.

Our secret to beating the Wheat Kings that year was actually their goalie: Ron Hextall. Hextall's temper in junior was way worse than it was when he played in the NHL. When he got older and made it to the NHL, he actually dialed it down, if you can believe it. But not when he was in junior. We only had to take a run at Ron once, and that would be it for the rest of the game. He would lose it and start swinging his stick at us the rest of the night. We knew that Ron liked to shoot the puck, too, so we would often dump the puck into the Wheat Kings zone and make Hextall rim the puck around the glass. Ron had a hard shot, so when he rimmed the puck around the glass, it would fly straight at his forwards' heads. While they were busy trying not to get their teeth knocked out by their own goalie, our forwards would be flying down from the blue line to hit them as soon as they had the puck. It wasn't the most sophisticated strategy, but it did the trick.

All in all, we had a good team in Saskatoon. We didn't win a Memorial Cup, but when I look at the guys who I played with and who coached me, and I see what they went on to accomplish—winning Stanley Cups, making All-Star games, representing Canada on the international stage—I'm immensely proud of my time there. And more than anything, I had a great time and grew as a person, and that made it all worth it. But nothing can last forever, and after two years in Saskatoon, I was more than ready to see what would happen at the upcoming NHL Entry Draft. I just had one more stop to make along the way.

3

1985 World Juniors

During my second year with the Saskatoon Blades, my game really started to come together. Up until that point, I hadn't followed any kind of weight-training program. In my first year in junior, I didn't spend much serious time in the gym. And if I did go, I'd just do a beach-body workout—bench press, some arm curls—for a couple of minutes, and then I'd go play racquetball. But in my second year, I started to get more serious about weight training, and I immediately got stronger on the ice. I was a defenceman, but I was putting up solid offensive numbers. I finished the season with thirty-two goals and eighty-seven points in sixty-four games, which was enough for me to be named the top defenceman in the WHL at the end of the season.

People started to take notice of my game, and in December 1984, I was invited to the Team Canada camp for the upcoming World Junior Championship in Finland. I couldn't believe what an opportunity it was. I tried to think of how the crowds in Saskatch-ewan would compare to the ones on an international stage, and I began to daydream about skating in front of them with the Cana-dian maple leaf on my chest.

I entered the camp full of energy. I was happy just to be there, but now that I had the chance in front of me, I wanted to seize it. So I put my head down and went to work. I made it all the way to the final cuts, when the coaching staff unexpectedly called me into their office. Sherry Bassin, the general manager, and Terry Simpson, the head coach, were there. As I walked into the small coaches' office, I was terrified. I figured they were going to break it to me that I was being sent home. Instead, Terry looked at me and said, "If you're going to make this World Junior team, you're going to have to play forward."

I was shocked. I had never played forward in my life up until that point. But I didn't hesitate. I said, "I'll play wherever you want me to play." I told them I would go over as a trainer if it meant I could take the flight to Finland and not the one back to Saskatoon.

Once that was settled, Terry Simpson piped up with one other condition for me joining the team. "You need to get a haircut," he said. "If you get a haircut before you get on the team bus, you can come to Finland." I wasn't surprised to hear that from a Western league coach like Terry. This was the 1980s, so I had a mullet; my hair was touching my name on the back of my jersey. Back then, a lot of guys like Terry had this thing about wanting everyone and everything on the team to be on the same page, the same way that Brent Sutter or Lou Lamoriello do today.

When I think back on it, I realize that Terry was probably laugh-ing under his breath when he said that. Sherry later told me that, after I left the office, he turned to Terry and asked, "What if he says no?" They didn't have to worry, though. I didn't want to risk missing the cut, so I found a barber in Belleville and got that haircut that same day.

Training camps for national teams are unique. The level of talent in the room is incredible, and you know that not everyone has a shot at making the team. Looking back, I'm amazed at the players who didn't make it to that 1985 team—Todd Gill, Joe Nieuwendyk, Gary Roberts, and even Patrick Roy were among the guys who got cut. We were all about the same age. It just came down to the fact that we had so much talent in camp and not everyone could make the team. Years later, Roberts and I were talking, and I told him the story of how I moved from defence to forward at the training camp. He looked at me with this odd expression and said, "So I got cut because they moved you from defence to forward?" Gary was the last cut from the team as a left wing—the position I took. He shook his head and repeated, "I got cut for a defenceman?"

Anytime you get to play for Canada as a part of the national team, you form an instant bond with the other players. The intensity in the one or two months you spend together is unlike any other experience. That year, we came together the moment we got off the plane and saw the conditions we had to deal with. When we arrived in Finland, it was mid-December, so for twenty-two and a half hours a day, the country was in total darkness. None of us had ever experienced anything like that before. When we first arrived, we didn't even go to Helsinki. Instead, we piled onto a bus that took us to a little town up in the bush.

Some of the guys missed being home for Christmas. Not me, though. A few years earlier, we'd started to have our Clark family Christmas in July. In December, my brothers and I were all playing different levels of hockey and going in different directions because we were in the middle of our seasons. We might be travelling and only get back home late on December 24, with no time to prepare. Or we'd be home for Christmas Day but would have to leave early on the morning of December 26. July was the only time of the year when everybody was home. So that's when we would all get together at our family cottage at Greenwater Lake Provincial Park and have a full turkey dinner. The whole thing was done for my mom's sanity. She got so excited when she could everybody together at the same time, and whenever that happened, she would label it Christmas, even if it was in July. It was fine by me. Besides, who turns down a turkey dinner, even in July? So being away for December made no difference to me—I was there to play the best hockey I could, without any distractions to hold me back.

Our training camp wasn't anything like the ones that you hear about today. We were all staying in little cabins that the Canadian organization had rented for us so that we could practise and prepare without distraction. These days, Hockey Canada takes food over for our athletes, and the players' nutrition is closely monitored the entire time they're there. They have private chefs who plan out every meal. I swear we ate green eggs and ham one morning. It was just like *Rocky IV*. We were in the middle of the Finnish mountains and we couldn't find trouble if you tried. All we could do was play hockey and hang out.

I didn't get to see much of Helsinki or Turku, the other city where we played games. When we broke camp and moved the team to Helsinki, we stayed at a hotel way outside of town. My older brother, Donn, had flown over to watch the tournament, and I was constantly hearing from him how much fun it was out on the town. But while he was living it up, we were out in the middle of nowhere. It was the right place for us to be, though. At the end of the day, we were there to play hockey, so it didn't really matter where we stayed.

We were scheduled to open the tournament against the Swedes. Before the game, we decided to go watch their practice to see what we'd be up against. We weren't there long before we started to think to ourselves, "There's no way we're going to be able to even touch those guys." I'd watch them practise and see how effortlessly and smoothly they moved the puck around. We all looked at each other with expressions that said, "We can't do that."

But that's why you play the games—to see if your best is better than someone else's. The Canadian system at that time was north–south, with lots of puck movement between the defence and forwards, and we relied on intimidation to a certain extent. The European system was more about puck possession. We had a big team and everybody could play physical. But even the guys who played a grind-it-out style had smooth hands. Despite the Swedes' skills, our tournament started off exactly as we'd planned, as we rolled over them, 8–2. After that, we shut out Germany 6–0 before beating the United States 7–5 a couple of days later.

Things were going incredibly well, and we didn't have any plans to slow down. Everyone was stepping up. On defence, Bobby Dollas was leading the way. Bobby had been with the Winnipeg Jets all year, but he'd only played a few games. Since he wasn't playing all that much, the Jets sent him to the national team to play with us at the World Juniors. He was named to the World Junior All-Star team that year. Our goalie, Craig Billington, was also unbelievable for us in that tournament. He stood on his head game in and game out. I don't think we allowed a shorthanded goal the whole tournament, and that usually speaks to the quality of your goaltending.

The 1985 World Juniors was also my introduction to players from other countries whom I would get to know quite well over the course of my NHL career. Finland's Esa Tikkanen was already trash-talking guys as a teenager. There's no doubt he had a really good tournament—he was the leading scorer that year—but he never shut up about it the whole time. And watching Czechoslovakia's Michal Pivonka play, I thought he was going to be like Gretzky. He was simply awesome, and he had the puck every time he was on the ice—I thought he was going to be a ten-year, one-hundred-point kind of guy.

In 1985, the World Juniors was a lot different than the tournament fans see today. The biggest difference was that there were no playoffs. It was a round-robin, and the championship rested on how many games you won and your goal differential—the difference between how many goals you scored and how few goals you allowed. Sometimes the medal winners were determined before you even got to your final game. But not in 1985. Heading into our final game, both Canada and Czechoslovakia had the same record: five wins and a tie. We had a goal differential of plus-thirty, while the Czechs were plus-nineteen. So they had to win the game outright to take the championship. All we had to do was tie and the gold medal was as good as ours.

There was nothing easy about that game. The Czechs had a 2–1 lead late in the third period. The coaches were trying all sorts of things to keep us in the game, so that night I actually played most of the game back on defence. But with five minutes left in the third period, I was sent out on forward for a faceoff in the offensive zone. Brian Bradley took the draw, I was in front of the net, and Adam Creighton was on the other wing. As Brian got control of the puck off of the draw, I backed away from the faceoff to the other hash mark. Everyone was focused on the puck, so I was able to drift back and get into a perfect shooting position. Brian read the play perfectly. He fed me a beautiful pass through traffic, and I one-timed the puck home for the tying goal. The bench erupted into cheers. But when we settled down, we remembered that we still had to make it through the final minutes of the game. Luckily, we were able to shut the door and keep the score even until the final buzzer sounded.

Although we'd tied the game, we couldn't celebrate just yet. The Soviet Union and Finland were yet to play, and there was an outside chance that the result would affect our chances for the gold medal. If the Soviet Union were to throw the game and allow Finland to score a ton of goals, it would mean that Finland would win the championship instead of us. Assuming everyone played legit, though, the tie that we'd just earned would be all we needed. Thankfully, the Soviets ended up beating Finland, 6–5, and Team Canada had won the gold medal.

One of my favourite parts of the tournament was that, at the end of every game, the winning team's national anthem was played. As I took my place along the blue line and threw my arms over the shoulders of the teammates beside me, I was overcome as we listened to "O Canada" play and watched the maple leaf raised to the rafters. The greatest thing about playing sports—not just hockey—in Canada is that you can make lifelong friends, the sort of people who, the moment you run into each other, you're thick as thieves, even if you haven't talked for ten years. If you're fortunate enough to play on teams that actually win something, whether it be a Stanley Cup or a World Juniors, your connections are even stronger because you share that success. Sports lets you form a bond that no other thing I know of can give you.

Our captain at the World Juniors that year was Dan Hodgson. Before the tournament, we were bitter enemies because he played with our major rival, Prince Albert. Years after the tournament, Dan called me to say that he was going to be passing through Toronto while I was there. It was decades after we'd played in Finland together, but the connection was still there. That's the beauty of sports.

Oddly enough, although we'd won the tournament, there wasn't much media coverage. None of the major Canadian outlets had bothered to send over a dedicated crew or reporters for the tournament. Just one Canadian reporter, a guy from Hamilton, was there. He said the tournament basically paid for his cottage, because when we started winning games and it looked like we might have a shot at the gold, all of a sudden the newspapers wanted coverage but nobody had any reporters in Finland. So all the media in Canada—especially the newspapers from the hometowns of the guys on the team—started paying this guy to freelance stories. When we got back to Canada, it was different: a nice reception awaited us at the airport. But after talking to the reporters there briefly, I got back on a plane for my connecting flight back to Saskatoon.

Instead of one great big party to celebrate the gold medal, the teams across the WHL held receptions and pregame ceremonies for all the players in the league who had been part of Team Canada. So, for the next few weeks, even when I was a playing for the visiting team, I would take part in the festivities. The most memorable was during one of our games in Calgary, when the fans gave us a standing ovation as we stood at centre ice. As I stared out at the applauding Calgary fans—people who might be cheering against me for the rest of the night—I realized the effect that hockey players have on Canadians.

While we were playing in Finland, we weren't thinking in "I" terms. It wasn't about our individual story, stats, or impact—it was about what we could do as a team to win the game. And that resonates with people. As a teenager, though, you don't see that bigger picture until you're signing autographs at a tournament in Swift Current, Saskatchewan, and then the sudden realization is overwhelming. You recognize that you've become part of something much bigger and that you have a responsibility to live up to it and do justice to your team, your fans, and your country. It was both thrilling and exhausting, so I was looking forward to getting back to my regular day-to-day routine.

I landed in Saskatoon and immediately joined the Blades for a three-game road trip. I literally got off the plane and walked onto the bus that took us to games in Calgary, Medicine Hat, and Lethbridge. I played all three games in four days, and then I got deathly sick with the flu. I was so run-down from playing in the World Juniors, the travel back from Finland, and the intense road trip, all without a break.

When I got over the flu bug, I noticed that I was playing at a higher level than I ever had before, all thanks to playing with and against the best junior players on the planet. Anytime you get to play the game at an elite speed, it helps you. You get used to practising and playing at a faster pace and seeing and feeling the game more quickly. You go back to the WHL and you are able to think about the game more effectively, and that translates into results.

Playing forward during the tournament had been incredibly useful, too. When I got back to the Blades, I played roughly 90 percent of the rest of our games back on defence. But I'd had a chance to see the game from an entirely different perspective, and I'd done it at one of the highest levels possible for me. Those insights were invaluable when I went back to playing defence regularly. More important, after playing in the World Juniors, I realized that the greatest players can slow the game down. In a situation where a regular player would panic and make a mistake, the great players go, "One . . . two," and then make the right play. It's hard to create that sort of mindset—you have to have the skill and talent on your team to practise at that kind of pace. But that's exactly what I was able to do at the World Juniors. Having that level of talent around me challenged me and forced me to become a better player. It was exhilarating, and I wanted more of it.

• • •

As I looked ahead to the rest of my season with the Blades, the next thing I had to do was decide who would be my agent for the upcoming NHL draft. As soon as I'd started with the Blades the year before, I'd begun talking to just about every agent out there, guys like Bill Watters, Norm Caplan, and Herb Pinder. Before my second season with the Blades had started, I'd opted to go with Caplan. But just as the season was getting under way, Norm passed away suddenly. So I put the brakes on everything and told all the agents who were trying to represent me that I had done enough talking. I would make my decision at the end of the season. I wanted to be left alone for the winter—no more dinners or phone calls or meetings.

When the time came to finally choose, I decided to sign with Don Meehan. In 1985, he wasn't yet one of the major agents in the sport. But I liked him, and I made a gut call with my parents' help. I had seen that a lot of agents considered their work on behalf of athletes to be a sideline or a subset of their bigger overall agency. But for Don, this was his career. I informed him of my choice just before the draft, and I never regretted that decision. As he went on to become a major figure in the player agent world, Don Meehan remained a major part of my career, as well as one of my best friends.

Since I'd left Kelvington, my dream had been to go to the NHL, but I was a realist. I knew that nothing was guaranteed—you never know you've made it until you've actually made it. But at this point in my life, the dream was closer to becoming reality than it ever had been. I had won the gold medal at the juniors, I was having a great season in Saskatoon, and I had an agent and family who supported me the whole way. I was ready for the draft and whatever my next step would be.

4

Welcome to the NHL

The 1985 NHL draft marked the first time the draft would be held outside of Montreal. And since 1980, every player who had been drafted into the NHL had heard their name called in the historic Forum. But on June 15, 1985, I found myself instead at the Metro Toronto Convention Centre.

Draft day is an emotional roller coaster. When you enter the building, your future is still uncertain. But when you leave, your path forward is suddenly much clearer. Going into that day, I had been in meetings with New Jersey, Pittsburgh, and a few other teams. All the organizations that I spoke with had seemed very interested in me. There were pros and cons to each, but even after talking to each one, I still had no idea who was going to draft me.

When the draft began, the stands were packed, and I was wedged in the middle of it all in a seat beside my mom, my dad, and my agent, Don Meehan. As John Ziegler, the president of the NHL at the time, stepped up to the podium to open the proceedings, a nervous calm quieted the arena. There was some scattered applause as the Toronto Maple Leafs were announced, and then everything went still and the spectators craned forward to hear the Leafs make the first-overall pick in the draft. I sat stock-still as the voice of Gerry McNamara, the Leafs' general manager, came over the speakers and made the official announcement: "The Toronto Maple Leafs are very happy to select Wendel Clark from Saskatoon."

As soon as McNamara had finished speaking, the building erupted in cheers and applause. I was thunderstruck. I rose from my seat slowly, completely overwhelmed. As people reached to shake my hand, I just kept looking from side to side, trying to figure out how to get out of the stands. When I realized I was penned in, I just tapped the shoulder of the guy in front of me and sidestepped over the seats to get past him and down to the floor.

The CBC was televising the draft, and before I could even get my bearings, the famed sportscaster Don Wittman appeared in front of me, wielding a microphone. As I walked towards the podium, I had to field questions from Don every step of the way. I barely remember the answers I gave—I was so focused on just putting one foot in front of the other and making it to the stage without tripping. At one point, I accepted a Leafs sweater that Gord Stellick shoved into my hands. Good thing I took it, too, because as soon as I'd left the stage, I had my photo taken more times than I can count, the most memorable being the one of Leafs owner Harold Ballard with his arm thrown around me as he grins from ear to ear. The rest of the event was a blur of congratulations, thank-yous, and handshakes. When I finally came up for air, I went back to my family and Don to recover. I spent the day with them, and then, later that night, I went out with Dave Manson and all the other young guys from the WHL who'd been at the draft. It was an honour to be selected first overall, and I knew that there would be a lot of change to come. But for the rest of that night, I was still just a junior hockey player, out with his friends to celebrate the fact that we were going to have a chance to keep playing hockey.

• • •

Following the draft, I went back to Saskatoon for a typical summer. I played ball, worked out, and come September, I went to the Saskatoon Blades training camp to start skating. I was going to be taking off for Leafs camp soon, and I wanted to make sure that I was in the best shape possible and that I had a chance to work off some of the summer rust before I entered the big leagues. The days and weeks flew by, and it wasn't long before I found myself back in Toronto for my first training camp.

I walked into the Gardens on the first day of camp completely in awe. I looked up at the banners hanging from the rafters, and I thought about how much history had taken place on the ice in front of me. Things only got better when I walked into the Leafs' dressing room and saw a number 17 sweater hanging in my stall. I had never asked for the number 17. I wore 22 in Saskatoon, but that was Rick Vaive's number, and I figured he didn't want to give it up. And seeing as how he was the captain of the Leafs, I wasn't about to ask! Someone mentioned that 17 was Dicky Duff's old number, and that was good enough for me.

For years, the idea of my joining the NHL had seemed so far away, but here it was, finally becoming a reality. I couldn't wait to make my mark. To do that, though, I told myself that the best thing I could do when I arrived in Toronto was just to be myself—to work hard, be a good teammate, and play my style of game. I figured that the Leafs had drafted me for a reason, and that they expected me to be the player and person I had been to that point. I didn't have to become someone I wasn't.

The team's plan was for me to play as a left-winger. Throughout training camp, we tried out a couple of different systems—I filled in on defence after we lost some guys to injury, and I played the point a bit on the power play. Nothing quite clicked, though, and so I fully committed to learning my new role as a forward. It suited me fine—I liked the idea of flying into the corner to mix it up with a defenceman, and I was excited to be in the thick of the action.

Of course, playing forward meant that I would be going up against a lot of big right defenceman on other teams, and given my style of play, that meant something was bound to happen. Bob McGill—or Big Daddy, as we called him—wanted to make sure I could handle myself. He had looked over my junior stats and had seen a lot of penalty minutes there, so he had decided to see just how tough the rookie was. So on the second day of camp, during a scrimmage, he took a run at me and we both immediately threw down our gloves and started trading punches. When the fight ended, we were laughing, and I said to my friend Russ Courtnall, "Russ, you do realize I went first overall? I'm not looking for the tough-guy job." It didn't matter to Bob, though. Thirty seconds later, he came at me and we were fighting again. And when we were finished, we just grabbed our gear and lined up for another faceoff. It was business as usual.

We had a great group in Toronto in my first year in the league. We had so many first-round draft picks playing on the team that year that we were basically a glorified overage junior team. Russ Courtnall, Gary Leeman, Todd Gill, Dan Hodgson, Jeff Jackson, Gary Nylund, Jim Benning, Kenny Wregget, Allan Bester, and I were all under twenty-two. We thought Rick Vaive, who was twenty-six, was old and that Borje Salming, at thirty-four, was ancient.

Salming was as tough as they come, and he was the most talented guy I ever played with. Borje entered the league in 1972, so he had already played thirteen seasons by the time I got to Toronto. But when we were skating laps, he could blow by me. The other young guys on the team all experienced the same thing—none of us could touch him. We used to wonder to ourselves what Borje must have been like a decade earlier.

Borje once went down south on a ten-day holiday with Harold Ballard where he did nothing but walk in the sand and relax for a week. Most guys would come back from that kind of downtime soft and tanned and out of touch. But in his first game back, Borje was named the first star. He had no body fat, and he didn't have to do anything to keep himself fit. In fact, he could barely do a bench press in the weight room. But when he had the puck, I could never lift his stick to take the puck off of him. When he had the puck, it was his, and he could do what he wanted with it.

Although most of us trained hard back then, the league was still old-school in a lot of ways. Smoking was still allowed in the dressing rooms, so whenever a new player showed up, the trainers would put out a spittoon and an ashtray in their locker stall. Some guys smoked, others dipped tobacco, and a few did both. I was used to it. When I was a kid, parents would smoke in cars when they drove me and my teammates to hockey games. And at some of my games in the old arenas out west—places like the barns in Saskatoon or Prince Albert—parents and fans would light up in the concourse between periods until the smoke was so thick that you couldn't see the top row of seats in the arena. I left all the smoking and dipping to the other guys, though, and stuck to my usual Coca-Cola and Gatorade.

The few short weeks of training camp opened my eyes to what life in the NHL would be like. It was a whirlwind, and I might have been carried away by it all had it not been for my fantastic billets at the time. My birthday is in late October, so I was still eighteen when the 1985–86 season got under way. To help with the transition from junior hockey to the NHL, the Leafs arranged for their rookies to live with billets in the city, ensuring that all of us had our own room, three square meals a day, and anything else we might need as we got used to the city. I lived with Peter Zezel's parents, Peter Sr. and Valerie. Peter Jr. was a year older than me, and he was playing with the Philadelphia Flyers, so I lived with his parents in Scarborough for the year. Living with the Zezels was great, because they knew the lifestyle of a hockey player better than anyone. During the weeks, they would help me with my laundry, feed me incredible meals, and make sure I was well rested, and they would come to the occasional Leafs game, especially if the Flyers were in town. On the weekends, they understood that I sometimes had to blow off steam. If I was going to run with the boys on the weekend, I would tell Peter and Valerie on Friday night that I would see them Monday morning, and then I'd crash at Russ's condo at the Palace Pier for a couple of nights.

I was grateful to be placed with such kind, warmhearted people, though I didn't billet with the Zezels for all that long. At the end of my first season, I moved into my own place on Madison Avenue, where I would live for the next eight years and where the kitchen of the nearby Madison Pub was a poor substitute for home-cooked meals in the Zezel family dining room. As a young player entering the league, my focus was entirely on hockey; I managed to completely forget about how I would have to adjust to the move to a big city. I was lucky, though, because, in my mind, the change is actually harder if you go from a city to a small town. In the city, everything you need is right at your fingertips. If you grow up there and then move to a small town, you realize very quickly that there's less to do, and fewer people to do it with. At the same time, the most important thing you have in a small town is your community. In a city, you can disappear into the crowds of people and no one pays you any mind. In the moments when I felt overwhelmed by the rapid pace of what was going on around me, I was thankful for having people like the Zezels, as well as my family back home, to keep me grounded.

● ● ●

There was a lot of buzz around my first game of the season. Being the first-overall draft pick might have been a personal honour, but it came with a lot of expectations. The fans, media, and team executives were all looking to me to make an immediate impact. If I didn't, there were bound to be questions. I continued to tell myself I just had to play my style of game, and that everything would follow from that. My confidence was on point, but it took some time for the results to show.

We started that season on the road against the Boston Bruins, and we lost, 3–1. I don't remember much about what happened during the game, but I will never forget what happened afterwards. Right after the end of the game, my centreman, Bill Derlago, was traded to the Bruins for Tom Fergus. So as the team got ready to leave, Derlago stayed behind in Boston while Tom Fergus hopped on the plane and came back with us to Toronto. I had only played in the NHL for sixty minutes, but already I was witnessing the business side of the league.

The next game was much of the same as we dropped our home opener to the Quebec Nordiques, 4–0. I didn't score my first NHL goal until the third game of my rookie season. We were playing Chicago—Murray Bannerman was in net for the Blackhawks—and I scored two goals. As a young player, you like to imagine that your first NHL goal will be one for the highlight reels, where you fire the puck bar down. But my goals weren't quite that pretty. They were both goal mouth scrambles, garbage goals that I scored by hanging around the crease, looking for something to happen. But I didn't care—I soon learned that most people were interested in *how many* goals you scored, not how you scored them. Besides, I'd always felt that a stat was only good if it helped the team, so the best thing about my first two goals was that they helped us earn our only win in the first ten games of that season. As good as scoring felt, winning felt better.

With that monkey off my back, I could let loose and get into a rhythm, and after that, things started to take off. The team started clicking, and I started to find ways to put the puck in the back of the net. And as we found success on the ice, we became closer as a team off of it. A lot of us young guys on the team were the same age, so not only were we working together on the ice, but we were hanging out together every day, too. I'd never had so much fun. Because we were in the Campbell (now Western) Conference that year, we travelled long distances a lot, from Los Angeles to Edmonton to Detroit, and everywhere in between.

The old Norris Division had some of the best road cities. Places like Chicago and St. Louis were a lot of fun to visit and play in. The one road city I never really liked was New York. Maybe it was the small-town guy in me, but I felt that it was so big that I never knew where I was going or what I was doing. And unlike a lot of guys, I never did like playing Madison Square Garden. While I had a few good games there, I often found the ice to be awful. The whole place just felt off to me—it didn't feel like an authentic rink. To start, I found it weird to go up to the sixth floor to play a hockey game. Every time I walked in, I thought the place smelled like elephants from the circus. The arena was dark, too, so the seats weren't visible. And on top of all that, sometimes, during the pregame skate, there would be pylons on the ice to warn us that the ice hadn't fully set in certain spots; Madison Square Garden was the busiest building in the NHL in terms of hosting concerts and other non-hockey events, and it was also the home of the Knicks. That being said, there was fantastic energy at every game in New York—we were hated whenever we played there.

Another thing about New York: in most cities, we could get a decent pregame meal without much trouble, but we often played the Rangers on Sundays, and finding a restaurant in Manhattan that was open for lunch in the mid-1980s seemed impossible. Some guys would be so desperate, they'd end up eating at McDonald's a few hours before the puck dropped. But those sorts of experiences brought us together. Teams that travel well together, play well together. It's as simple as that.

My first roommate on road trips with the Leafs was our goalie,

Don Edwards. Don was a veteran, and he was very friendly. I imagine that's why I was paired up with him—the coaching staff probably figured he'd keep an eye on me. I enjoyed Don's company, and he was a great guy to get to know. Later, I started rooming with other guys, like Russ Courtnall, Todd Gill, Dave Ellett, and Darryl Shannon. I particularly enjoyed rooming with Russ, since Russ and I were the same age. It didn't matter who I roomed with, though, we managed to have a good time. Sometimes, a little too much of a good time.

One night in my first year, we were all out as a team after a game in Minnesota. We were staying in the Marriott hotel by the airport on the edge of town, and the coaching staff had imposed a curfew—they were disappointed that we'd been on a losing streak lately. But the threat of punishment wasn't enough to stop us. The whole team missed the curfew, and the night wasn't over when we got back to the hotel. As we headed back up to our rooms, somebody noticed that there was a phone inside the elevator. The next thing we knew, someone had ripped the phone off and was carrying it back to his room like a trophy. We weren't exactly subtle about it all, and it wasn't long before the hotel staff was phoning our coach, Dan Maloney, to let him know what was going on. Dan was livid, and he started going room to room to check on who was out after curfew. Of course, not a single one of us was in our room. Russ was rooming with Brad Smith at the time, and as Russ walked into his room, he yelled to Brad, "I made it!" He looked up and came face-to-face with Maloney, who was just about to exit their room when Russ and Brad showed up at the door.

We half-thought Dan was going to kill Russ—Brad was hanging off Dan's back, trying to keep him from getting at Russ. Dan wasn't someone you wanted to be mad at you. Needless to say, the team wasn't invited back to the hotel after that night. So, instead of staying out by the strip mall, the next time we were in town, we got to stay downtown at the brand-new Marriott hotel. Somehow we managed to turn a broken telephone and a near fistfight into a sweeter hotel deal.

Not every night could be like that, though. One thing I learned quickly as young player was that you need to pick the right time to go out and have some fun. It all boiled down to knowing yourself, knowing your team, and knowing the situation. In our day, if only one or two guys had a late night and looked a little rougher for it the next morning, they'd stand out. If everybody went out together, you didn't notice the difference the next morning. We were a team, so in our minds, we did things together or not at all.

There were lots of ways we made everyone feel like a part of the team. Before I broke into the NHL, I'd heard rumours about hazing. But by the time I arrived as a rookie in 1985, it seemed to be dying down. I never got hazed. In fact, I don't remember anyone getting initiated that year. There were jokes about it, of course, and the veterans liked to try to mess with our heads. At one point, somebody mentioned something to me about being shaved. I replied, "Well, you can try. But if I go down, I'm taking at least six guys with me. So, go ahead. Just know there's going to be a fight." Nobody decided to try me.

Hazing never made any sense to me. On a team, you want people to feel comfortable as quickly as possible; that's the way that you get the best results from everyone. We didn't want people to feel scared right off the bat. So we found other ways of helping the team come together and making each person feel like a part of it, none of which required anything humiliating. Being embarrassed never gets anyone anywhere. It doesn't make a team better, and you never knew exactly what another guy was thinking or feeling, whether he might be holding a grudge. Hazing was something that belonged to the old-school era in sports, but we didn't need it. The tradition I preferred was the rookie dinner: each year, the rookies would pay for the veterans to eat at a nice restaurant, and the only thing that got hurt those nights was the rookies' wallets.

Of course, we still knew how to have fun. Humour was one of the best tools we had for bringing the team closer together. Russ Courtnall, along with being a great roommate and friend, is also one of the funniest guys I've ever met. And in my first year with the Leafs, did we ever need that. We didn't exactly start the 1985–86 season the way we wanted. After the first sixteen games of the season, we only had one win, and it had come on the road against Chicago. The team was in poor spirits, and it seemed like nothing on the ice would lift them. So Russ took it upon himself to ease the tension with some practical jokes.

The towels that we used in the shower at the Gardens were all white. Russ's brilliant idea was to put baby powder and Vaseline in every single one of them. Someone was bound to hit the showers after the game, and Russ figured that seeing them covered in gel and powder would be a great pick-me-up, whether we were celebrating or feeling low.

Things didn't quite go the way that Russ planned, though. He set up the towels just before we went out for our warm-up skate, assuming that no one would use them until after the game was over. But our coach, Dan Maloney, decided that he needed a shower just before the game started. Dan got out of the shower, grabbed a towel, and started to walk through the dressing room. By the time he realized that he was covered in baby powder and Vaseline, it was too late—he was already in the middle of the dressing room. We didn't know how to react. On the one hand, we were in a major winless streak, and we didn't want Dan to catch us laughing, because we knew we couldn't afford for him to be even angrier at us. But on the other hand, the guy we were supposed to be taking more seriously than anyone else was standing in front of us, looking like a lumpy snowman. We might have been able to hold it in, but that same day, one of the coaches—apparently having the same idea about team bonding as Russ—had cut the feet out of Dan's dress socks so that, when Dan pulled on his sock, the tube would just shoot up his leg.

Needless to say, we barely held it together as Dan stormed out of the dressing room to wash off the baby powder.

There we were, nearly a quarter of the way through the season with barely a win to our name, and we were still cracking up together. It wasn't that we didn't care about winning hockey games—we cared about that more than just about anything. But we needed a way to get out of our heads and stay loose in the dressing room if we were ever going to be able to turn things around on the ice. Looking around the dressing room at those guys, all of whom were keeping their cool and having fun even in that rough patch, I knew that we were going to be able to turn things around.

Russ and I were very tight. When we were teammates, I told him that if a scrum ever broke out after a whistle, he should count to three. If I wasn't there by then, the only reason he'd be on his own would be that I was off fighting somebody else. In my first year, Russ and I were both single, so we often didn't have anywhere to go after practice. Instead of hustling out of the arena, we'd stay after practice and shoot pucks. We were usually the last two guys to leave the dressing room every day. One day, we decided to take all that spare time on our hands and put it to good use. We were sitting in Guy Kinnear's training room, and we decided to load up all the blow dryers with baby powder. We knew that no one would be in the showers that day, but we figured we would have everything set up for the next morning, and by that time no one would be able to pin it on us. We were giggling at just the thought that someone would come in, turn on the hair dryer, and *poof,* get a face full of baby powder. We had everything loaded and were getting ready to leave, when in walked Harold Ballard.

Harold was not someone we wanted to mess with. He owned the Toronto Maple Leafs, and his sense of humour was worlds apart from that of a couple of teenage boys like Russ and me. Harold walked into the bathroom, where he started looking at himself in the mirror. He had this beautiful suit on, and he was looking at his hair and primping himself. Then he reached for the blow dryer. I grabbed Russ's leg and started saying, "No! No! No!" We watched in absolute terror as Harold hit the power button, instantly covering his entire head in baby powder.

We were laughing and shitting ourselves at the same time. Harold turned towards us, and all you could see was his red mouth, because he was completely white. There was nowhere for us to run because there was only one door in and one door out of the room. You have never seen two guys in their late teens almost have a heart attack like we almost did right then. We were whiter than Harold Ballard at that moment. Ballard took off his glasses, and there was an outline of white around his eyes. Then he said to us, "Now *that's* a good one," before leaving the room.

● ● ●

Although we were having fun off the ice, we always brought our focus back to what really mattered: winning hockey games. Our coaches pushed us—they knew we were young guys and that we were competitive. But still, no matter how hard anyone pushed me, they could never be as hard on me as I was on myself. Early in my career, I had a habit of throwing up a lot before games. I think I threw up before half of my games that year alone, all from being so wound up before we hit the ice. I wasn't getting sick from nerves—I was winding myself up. To get ready for a game, I would get myself on edge, trying to amp myself up and push myself into a competitive zone, hoping to be able to play a big game. I'd be visualizing the game—what might happen, who I would face, what I needed to do. I'd get caught up in all the possibilities and what-ifs, completely wrapped up in my thoughts. But when I did that, it ramped my nerves up and took away my appetite, and the next thing I knew, I was in the bathroom stall in the dressing room, heaving.

Later in my career, I came to realize that I couldn't keep doing that to myself game after game—it was just too exhausting. But even as a veteran, if it was a do-or-die playoff game or a big matchup, sometimes my body would sense that energy and I would end up throwing up again. As a young man, though, I didn't think there was anything all that wrong with what was happening. I thought it was the only way I could keep my edge, and I wanted every competitive advantage I could find.

About halfway through my rookie season, things started to change for the better. Our wins started to come a little more frequently—a sign of us playing better as a team—and I was scoring goals more and more frequently. Most of my thirty-four goals came in the second half of the season.

There was one reason for my new success in the later part of that season: I was finally figuring out how to play forward. Our coaching was different back then. As a rookie, most of what I was being taught was general—special-teams plays, positional systems, that sort of thing. I didn't receive a whole lot of instruction as far as personal development was concerned. Often, the best way to learn something is just by doing it, and I simply hadn't played forward as much as I had played defence over the years. But game after game, I figured it out more and more. As the weeks went by, I wasn't just reacting to the play, I was becoming more aware and realizing where to be before I had to be there. Having been one for so long, I already knew how defencemen would respond in certain situations, like a dump-and-chase or a one-on-one rush. Where goalies were concerned, I had been trained for so long in how to keep the puck away from the goalie and out of the net, but the more I saw things from the other side, the more I was able to spot weaknesses and exploit those opportunities.

I may have only been a rookie, but I knew I couldn't rely on emotion alone to carry me through a career in the NHL. When push came to shove, I had to be able to actually play the game, and so learning the mechanics of how to play forward was invaluable. In my first training camp, a lot of the rookies or the guys who had played in Europe were unbelievable. Watching them play, you could see them wearing their hearts on their sleeves, going all out in every situation and letting their excitement, desperation, or exhilaration fuel their game. On the other hand, the guys who had a season or more in the NHL under their belts eased into camp. They recognized that the season was a marathon, not a sprint. By the time the three weeks of camp were up, it was usually those veteran NHL guys who were looking more focused, more skilled, and more practised.

A lesson like that is the sort of thing you could only learn by spending time in the league. Another one I learned as a rookie in the NHL was that every rink is different—this was especially true in the 1980s. For instance, in the old Memorial Auditorium in Buffalo, the visiting-team facilities were so small that we had to dress in two separate rooms. The coach would have to go back and forth between the two rooms to yell at us if he was mad. I'd be sitting with the other forwards, thinking to myself, "Please yell at the guys on defence and leave us alone!" Coaches usually had enough to shout about that they could spread it around, though.

The old Boston Garden was bad, too. The size of the dressing rooms wasn't too bad; it was the cockroaches and rats that made it tough. After our morning skate, we'd leave our gear in the dressing room. When we got into our gear for the pregame skate a few hours later, we'd have to shake everything before we put it on to make sure no cockroaches had snuck in there while we were away.

Not all the rinks were that rough, though. Much like Maple Leaf Gardens, the Montreal Forum felt like a shrine. The Forum might have been an old building, but it was immaculately kept. Every time I stepped onto that ice and saw how the red, white, and blue seats glistened under the bright arena lights, I felt like I was stepping into a cathedral. The seats were repainted every year to keep them looking fresh, and at the start of the season, the decades-old arena managed to look brand-new. On top of that, no other rink had an end-of-period siren like the Forum. Every time I heard it, I was taken back to when I was a kid, hearing it blare out of the TV set while I watched *Hockey Night in Canada*.

In December of my rookie year, the coaching staff shook things up a little bit and called up Steve "Stumpy" Thomas from our American Hockey League farm team in St. Catharines. Steve is a great example of perseverance and loving the game. He was never drafted, but he didn't let that stop him from making the Show. He was a late bloomer who needed time to develop, but he played hard and he was a great teammate. While he wasn't tall, Stevie was a stocky guy with a thick chest. We used to joke that his chest was too big for his body. Stumpy had already scored eighteen goals in only nineteen games while he bided his team in the AHL, and after joining the team in December 1985, he scored twenty goals in sixty-five games. That is pretty impressive stuff for an undrafted player.

As I hit my stride around the midway point of the season, I had really come to appreciate that you couldn't get by on emotion alone. Maintaining your focus and perspective is a key element over an eighty-game schedule. We all were seeing the value of that, and nothing demonstrated it better than the night of January 8, 1986. The Edmonton Oilers were in town that night, and we knew we were in for a big game. Edmonton was full of gunners—Paul Coffey, Mark Messier, Wayne Gretzky, and Grant Fuhr. They were the defending Stanley Cup champions, so as we got ready in the dressing room that night, we tried to focus on how to play the best game possible. I was particularly anxious to get back on the ice that night. It was my first game back from a broken foot, and Dan Maloney had put me back on the Hound Line to jump-start our offence. I knew—just like the rest of the guys in the room did—that if we gave in to any nerves or let our emotions get the better of us, the Oilers would roll right over us. We had to channel that emotion into our play on the ice and let that do the talking.

Well, we didn't just talk that night—we had a full-on shouting match. At the end of the second period, the game was already 6–5 in our favour. We still had a period to go, but if the game had ended there, it still would have been spectacular. The puck never stopped dancing, with the play moving nonstop from end to end and back again. I was clicking with Russ and Gary that night, and I managed to score a goal that was soon lost among the many others that followed it. But after I scored, I sat on the bench and told the guys around me, "Shoot the puck—everything is going in." From that point on, we just threw the puck at the net. We were used to seeing the Oilers score goal after goal, but we weren't quite as familiar with doing it ourselves.

When the final buzzer sounded, we had beaten the Oilers 11–9. Wayne Gretzky had a hat trick and three assists, and somehow we still managed to come out ahead. It helped that Miroslav Frycer had answered Gretzky with four goals for us. But it was far from a one-man effort. Every single guy had chipped in and done his part. There's no way we could have pulled out a win like that otherwise.

We were almost giddy in the dressing room after the game. We'd managed to keep our emotions in check and rise to the occasion, but when you got down to it, we were basically a bunch of junior-aged kids who had managed to overcome the powerhouse of the NHL. The coaches hated the game because it had been a defensive night-mare. But as players, we were feeling pretty good.

● ● ●

Although I was learning to score, I was also using my time to develop the other parts of my game. Having learned to fight in junior, that was another of my tools, one I didn't want to give up. I didn't want to step aside and let others wage my battles for me.

Of course, I didn't want to drop the gloves just for the sake of fighting. I couldn't—and wouldn't—start picking on guys and whal-ing on them for no good reason. Once I was in a fight, sure—I would go straight ahead, full bore, all pistons firing as I started swinging. But I wasn't a big guy, and I recognized that every player was differ-ent, with his own personality and fighting style. There were some I might do better against and some who'd get the better of me.

I was never worried about fighting the big guys. I would be on my guard in those situations, because I knew that whoever I was facing was bound to hit hard and be a tough customer. Instead, it was the smaller guys—the ones who were, say, my size—who gave me pause. Because if I wasn't careful, they could prove to be far tougher than I'd first expected. Just because a guy didn't fight often, it didn't mean he was a pushover.

One of my favourite teammates was Todd Gill. Todd was a defenceman on the Leafs in my first year, and he was a popular guy who got along well with everyone. He was one of the best team players around. I'm also convinced he was one of the best fighters in the league, pound for pound. Todd wasn't famous for fighting—in his fifteen games with the Leafs that year, he only racked up twenty-eight penalty minutes. But nothing scared Todd. He was only about 175 pounds soaking wet, but he was tough as nails and could handle himself in any situation. I watched opponents underestimate him, thinking they could push him or his teammates around without him stepping in to stop them. They couldn't have been more wrong.

One night in my rookie year, we were in Detroit, and I watched Todd step up to fight Joey Kocur. Joey had 377 penalty minutes that season alone, and as they squared off, everyone thought Todd was crazy. They figured he would last one or two punches and then be done. But Todd did more than hold his own, and as I watched him transform from the friendly team member to the fearsome fighter, I told myself I could never underestimate anyone.

I was never afraid of anyone in the league, but I did realize that I had to be constantly alert and aware of who was on the ice with me. That way, I felt prepared and able to respond to whoever was coming my way. Preparation and vigilance were the key—being caught by surprise was the danger. For the most part, though, I didn't have to worry about that. The toughest guys in the league were never the craziest ones. Most of the time, the enforcers were the most polite guys out there. They would skate up to you and simply say,

"We're going." Even someone as tough as Bob Probert was a good guy at heart. Fighting Probert was like booking a date. He'd skate up to you and say something not far from, "Excuse me, sir, we're going to fight tonight." And you didn't say no to Bob.

Learning how to prepare for a fight and adapt to setbacks took time. Harold Snepsts was a pain in my butt when I was young player, and he knew it, too. Harold was a big, strong veteran, and he would do anything to throw me off my game. Since he was so strong, he could tie me up in a scrum. It wasn't just me that he targeted, though. Harold was smart, and he knew how to get any guy off his game. It took me a while to get over my frustration with Harold's style of play. As a rookie, I was constantly fired up but had not yet figured out that, sometimes, stepping back and taking a cooler route is more effective. In those early days, I was all passion. One game in particular stands out. We were playing Detroit, and the game was being televised on *Hockey Night in Canada*, which meant there were cameras everywhere. Harold and I were mixing it up all game, and at one point I took a penalty because of it. I was so angry that I yelled at Harold the entire time I skated to the penalty box. I let fly with a barrage of f-bombs. What I didn't realize was that viewers were seeing a close-up of my face the entire time. And of course, my family back home in Kelvington was watching the game. The next day, my mom said that my grandma had asked her, "What is Wendel saying there?" My mom replied, "I don't think we're going to tell you what Wendel is saying there."

Dave Brown was another guy you had to watch out for. Dave was a tough lefty with an enormous reach. Sometimes Dave fought because it was his job. Other times he did it because he was mad. You didn't mind fighting Brownie when he was doing his job—those were the times when he was polite and respectful. But you didn't want to fight him when he was mad. That's when he went to a different level, and it could get dangerous.

I first met Dave when I was attending the Saskatoon Blades'

training camp as a thirteen-year-old. I was far from making the team at that time, but I would go to the camp just for the experience, and every now and then I would be put on the wing with him for a drill. Dave later went on to play junior with my older brother, Donn, in Yorkton. The first time I played with the Leafs in Philadelphia, I spotted Dave stretching right beside the red line at centre ice. I figured he had positioned himself there so he could stare us down or chirp us as we skated by and did our pregame drills. As I wheeled past centre, Brownie looked over at me and called out, "Clarkie, how's your brother doing?" I was stunned—here was a known tough guy whom I'd barely seen in the past five years, and he remembered my family. It was one of the happiest moments of my early career. I knew then that I wouldn't have to fight him that night unless something really bad happened on the ice, and I was thrilled to see how the guys on every team would put personal touches like that ahead of on-ice hostility.

I saw a lot of that sort of politeness and gentlemanly behaviour in my rookie year. It was a fantastic learning experience. Seeing the veterans, the stars, the enforcers, or the journeymen all carry themselves the same way was an important lesson for me. It reinforced the idea that no player was more important than any other, and that you had to respect the other guys on the ice, whether you were lining up beside them or across from them. But I wasn't very far into that first season before I saw the flip side of the coin. Sometimes, every attempt at mutual respect or politeness with a guy was bound to fail.

In my fifteen years in the NHL, to my mind, the craziest and meanest guy I ever faced was, without a doubt, Behn Wilson of the Chicago Blackhawks. The first time I fought Behn was during my rookie season. Partway through the game, I was on the ice, breaking out of our zone on a three-on-two. As we headed up ice, Wilson—who was trailing the play—skated over to our bench and speared Rick Vaive right in the guts. Rick must have done something earlier to really tick Wilson off. Rick wasn't even on the ice when it happened—he was sitting behind the bench. We didn't realize it had happened until the play was over and we made our way back to the bench. I was shocked. As the guys on the bench reacted to what had happened, I learned that you really didn't have to do much for Behn to find a reason to go after you. All you had to do was finish your check on Behn and he was going to lose it on you. I couldn't believe what a disrespectful move that had been, and so, later in the game, I ended up getting in a fight with him. I held my own, too, which was saying something, because Behn could be downright scary.

I fought Behn a number of times in games after that. I knew I was never going to scare him. Behn had played eight years in the league, and he had survived on straight intimidation, trying to scare the living shit out of opponents. I was fighting him when he was an older player, so I knew he was set in his ways. But I wasn't trying to intimidate him. I just couldn't sit by and watch players like Behn get away with things like spearing guys in the kidneys or cross-checking them in the face. That wasn't how I wanted to see the game played, and it got me fired up anytime I saw it happen. Physical play was an important part of my game, and I loved a challenge, so I never stepped down from a fight. And I was always ready to make sure that I backed up my teammates, whether that was with a goal or a fist.

● ● ●

My turnaround in my rookie season seemed to catch a few eyes, because in February, I was lucky enough to be selected as a member of the Campbell Conference team for the NHL All-Star Game. I was still a teenager at the time, so the opportunity to play beside the best players in the league had me so excited that I was literally counting down the days to the game.

The whole experience was awe-inspiring. I can barely recall the lead-up to the event. I just remember sitting in the dressing room be-fore the game and feeling like I was in the Edmonton Oilers dressing room. Glen Sather was coaching our team that year, and the Oilers were so good that the Campbell team was made up almost entirely of Oilers players. Except for Chicago's Doug Wilson on defence, the entire starting lineup was from Edmonton. The atmosphere was in-credibly friendly, though. All the guys were awesome and treated me well, even though I was younger and not a part of their usual crew.

The game itself was a ton of fun, too. I was having a blast, al-though it took me a little while to get the vibe of the game. Sather and the rest of my teammates got a kick out of the fact that I was trying to throw body checks. In an All-Star game. And it wasn't like I'd hit anyone forgettable (not that that's really possible in an All-Star game)—I hit Ray Bourque and I *tried* to hit Mario Lemieux. Luckily, both they and my team were laughing when I did it; the boys on the bench were having fun winding me up. After that, though, I settled into the pace and feel of the game a little more, and I realized that Sather had probably put me on the team exactly because he wanted to stir things up.

Sather was an intense coach, though, so his playfulness only went so far. In the third period, the score was close, so he decided to bench most of us and play only his Edmonton boys. Who says teams weren't trying to win the All-Star game back in the day? Sather didn't believe in taking a night off. So he shortened the bench and stuck with his Oilers to go for the win.

Nobody wants to be benched during an All-Star game, but I ad-mired Glen's competitiveness, and he had incredible hockey knowl-edge. After the game, I found myself beside him outside the dressing room. I expected to make a few seconds of small talk, but instead, Glen turned to me and said, "You're not going to last."

I was shocked; he'd caught me totally off guard and I didn't know how to respond. I walked away, trying to process what Glen had just said. I realized he wasn't trying to put me down; he was trying to warn me. In my first year in the NHL, I had been playing recklessly. I would throw my body around, tearing up and down the ice at full speed as I tried to bruise and bash my way through the other team. I didn't care if it hurt. I thought I was invincible. And when my physical play produced results—goals, assists, momentum changes—it made me want to go out and make another check. The more I hit, the better things went, and so the more I wanted to do it again.

Glen saw the way I played, and he knew there was no way I'd be able to keep going at that pace. He had the foresight that so many people, myself included, lacked. Fights can cause injuries or lead to problems later in a career. But many more injuries—mine in particular—come from hitting, not fighting. It doesn't matter what size you are, physical play will catch up with you one way or another, because dishing out a hit hurts your body almost as much as taking one. If you're caught carrying the puck in open ice with your head down, you can expect to have the air forced out of you when an opposing defenceman comes barreling across and nails you in the centre of your chest with his shoulder. But the guy who's doing the hitting, well, his shoulder still feels the impact of the weight of your entire body colliding with his. You're both going from twenty miles per hour to a dead stop in very little padding, and that has consequences. As a fan, that sort of check is what you love to see—it's exciting to watch. But as I found out—and as everyone else who plays in the NHL comes to realize—the body will eventually wear down.

As I left the All-Star weekend, that sort of thinking was only vaguely starting to come together in my mind, but I didn't consider just what it might mean. I was young and focused on what was immediately in front of me, not what was coming years down the line. The All-Star game had been a blast, and I was looking forward to bringing that energy back to the Leafs and seeing what we could do in the second half of the season.

As the spring drew near, things started to pick up for both me and the team. Every game, I could feel myself getting a little stronger and a little smarter, and I was scoring more frequently. Late in the season, I scored my thirty-second goal of the season, which was memorable only because it set a new Leafs record for goals scored by a rookie. After I scored, the record was announced over the loud-speakers at the Gardens. The fans started going crazy, and they even went so far as to give a standing ovation. While I was sitting on the bench, I turned and gave the crowd a wave. Then I turned back and said to Russ Courtnall beside me, "I'd rather fight than score any day." We chuckled as the noise from the crowd slowly quieted and the game resumed. As intense as all games are in the NHL, there was often stuff said on the bench that reminded us that we were still kids at heart.

We managed to earn a playoff spot by taking fourth place in our division that year. That meant we drew the Chicago Blackhawks in our opening, best-of-five round. The Blackhawks had won the Norris Division with eighty-six points, and we had squeaked into the playoffs with only fifty-seven. So when we beat Chicago in three straight games, the hockey world was shocked. We were thrilled, but we weren't surprised. We might have been young, but we were hungry and we knew we could hold our own. And we knew that we had beaten Chicago the last three times we'd faced them in the regular season. So while many around the NHL didn't give us a chance, we knew better. We brought that energy into the second round against the St. Louis Blues. We traded the lead in games throughout the series, but eventually, St. Louis knocked us out with a Game Seven win in their own barn, closing out my first season.

I was disappointed that our year had ended early, because I still had the energy to keep playing. I felt good physically, I wasn't mentally burned out, and, more than anything, I wanted to win. As I packed up my locker that year, I knew I would be back, and I told myself to remember what being kicked out of the playoffs felt like. I was determined to do everything I could to make sure that I'd never feel it again.

After the season ended, I headed back to Kelvington for some downtime. The weeks were filled with farm work and helping out my family, and the weekends were for baseball tournaments. I joined a team with the other junior and NHL guys in the area, like Joey Kocur, Barry Melrose, and Neil Clark. We had a tough team, that's for sure! Melrose was the catcher, my brother Donn played first base, I played shortstop and was the backup pitcher, and Joey Kocur played third base. Neil Clark, Kerry Clark, and Kelly Chase were in the outfield. And Trent Yawney would sometimes come down from Hudson Bay to play outfield. Brian Finch, a good farm guy, was our regular pitcher. Joey Kocur's cousin, Kory, and Kevin Kaminski rounded out the team.

You had to see Barry Melrose hit a ball to believe it. He could hit a ball harder than anyone I ever saw in my days playing baseball. And he could do it using a wooden bat. We were all using aluminum bats, but Barry preferred the old-school wooden ones. He would bat cleanup, and more often than not, he'd pound the ball over the fence. Sometimes we would stay on base and just watch the ball fly away, our jaws dropping at how far he'd hit it. The scariest thing was standing on third base when Barry was at bat. Donn said he was always worried he'd end up like Charlie Brown—knocked down with his clothes flying everywhere—if Barry ever hit a line drive down the third-base line.

People who came to watch us didn't come to see the team play, they came to watch Barry hit. On Sundays, people who never played baseball would still be at the ballpark, taking in the show. The crowd was even bigger when we held tournaments. Fans came out to cheer on the hometown team and enjoy the beer garden and barbeque. Everyone you knew would be there. As much as hockey was our entertainment in a small town in the winter, ball remained our fun for the summer.

Going home to Kelvington for the summer was the perfect way to rest and recover from the season. But even there, I couldn't totally get away from hockey. There is a roadside sign as you enter Kelv-ington that lists the names of all the local guys who went on to play pro hockey. For a little town of nine hundred people, it is amazing to see how many names are on that board. The sign is painted by hand, and it has to get updated on a regular basis—the weather does a number on it every winter. After my first season with the Leafs, my name was added to the sign. As I looked over the list of names, I noticed there was a guy named Lloyd Gronsdahl, who'd played briefly for the Bruins just at the start of the Second World War. When I asked my dad about him, he said Lloyd had had the best wrist shot around—and even better, he'd worn number 17.

After a couple of months of long, summer days of playing ball with the boys and catching up with people around town, I felt the usual itch to get back on the ice. I was ready to get to work. And so, come September, I packed up my things and headed back to the Saskatoon Blades' training camp to get prepped for my sophomore year with the Maple Leafs.

● ● ●

As I made my way from Saskatoon to Toronto for training camp, I looked forward to my second season in the NHL. I'm not a deep thinker, so I didn't reflect on what I wished had happened the year before. And despite what Glen Sather had said at the All-Star game, I wasn't about to change my style. My goal for 1986–87 was to be better than the year before and help the Leafs win, no matter what it took. The thought of another season with the Leafs got me thinking about the history of the team and my place within it. And at that time, thinking about the history of the Toronto Maple Leafs or the state of the team inevitably led you back to Harold Ballard.

I didn't know much about Ballard before I got to Toronto be-cause I hadn't followed the NHL very closely when I was growing up. It all seemed a long way away from Kelvington. If I had paid attention, though, I would have heard Harold's name over the years in just about any discussion of the Leafs, their successes, and their pitfalls. As the owner of the Leafs, Ballard was famous for being involved in every aspect of the team, whether the team liked it or not. And, of course, if I heard Harold's name, I also would have heard mention of King Clancy in the same breath.

Clancy was one of the first—and finest—guys I met in Toronto. He had an honorary office at Maple Leaf Gardens, and I never met anyone better at promoting the team. He was Mr. Positive, one of those guys who would tell anyone who would listen that the Maple Leafs were the greatest hockey organization there was. He and Harold Ballard were best friends, the last two guys left from a bygone era. The two of them would eat breakfast together every morning at the Hot Stove Lounge in the Gardens, and come game time, you would be sure to find them watching the game from their bunker at the end of the rink. King had had a role in every level of the game— he'd played, reffed, coached, and now he was an executive, one of the public faces of the Toronto Maple Leafs. I was in the NHL for just over a year before he passed away, and after that, in my second season, I found myself getting to know Harold Ballard a lot better.

After I joined the Leafs, I developed a great relationship with Harold. From the very first moment we met and I saw how he treated my mom and dad, to the media coverage about my injuries, I knew he had my back. At one point in my third year with the team, I got hurt, and it came out in the paper that Harold said I was "swinging the lead," an old saying that described someone who was pretending to be sick to get out of work. Right after that particular interview, Harold walked by me in the hallway and said, "I don't give a shit when you come back. Come back when you're healthy." I recognized that Harold was saying what he had to in order to stir up the media and make it appear as though he was lighting a fire under his players to keep them motivated. But I knew that Harold would let us do whatever we needed to play the best hockey we could.

Harold Ballard was a man of contradictions. He had struggled with his diabetes, but he also constantly had chocolates on him. Harold and King were once on a charter flight together, and as the two of them boarded, King turned to one of the stewardesses and said, "Don't give the old guy any chocolate—he's a diabetic." So when Harold asked for some chocolates, the stewardess told him he wasn't allowed. What she didn't know was that Harold was the one who had chartered the plane in the first place. So when Harold got off the plane, he cancelled his contract with the charter service right then and there and replaced it with another one that would let him eat his chocolate.

I also had a great relationship with Gord and Bob Stellick, who were with me through the whole Ballard era. They were great supporters, and they knew how to keep the ship afloat from day to day. Both were so good to me my first few years in the league. Anytime I had a question or needed something, they would help me take care of it. A few years later, at the start of the 1988–89 season, Gord, who by then was the general manager, really took care of me while we were negotiating my second contract with the Leafs. We had been discussing deal points over the summer, and we came to an agreement well before the season started. When we got to training camp, Ballard went up to Gord and said, "We have to do the Clark contract."

Harold expected that to be the start of the process. What he didn't know was that I'd already signed the contract. Gord thought he was going to be in shit because he had already done the deal and hadn't told Harold yet! Gord and the other guys working under Harold were all pretty young back then, so they were all learning on the job, just like I was. During one session in training camp, I was called off the ice and into Harold's office. When I got there, Gord took out a blank piece of paper with a line on the bottom. Harold signed one side of the line and I signed the other. And then Harold announced, "Okay, Wendel's done his contract now." We had to pretend that I was signing the deal right there, because Harold wanted to feel like every major contract was his doing. So there I was, sweating in full hockey equipment in the middle of a practice, signing a "contract" that was nothing more than two names on a piece of paper. It might not have held up in a court of law, but it did the trick, and it kept Gord out of the doghouse.

Say what you will about Harold Ballard, he really knew how to hold court. His headquarters were just behind the main office at the Gardens, and his apartment was right there as well. I found myself in Harold's apartment in the arena a few times. It wasn't very big—maybe four hundred square feet. He had a penthouse apartment in the building right next door, but he never stayed there. To Harold, Maple Leaf Gardens was house and home. If he was stressed, he would hit the hot tub in the dressing room. If he was hungry, he would go down to the Hot Stove and raid the fridge. And in the middle of the night, he sometimes walked up to the top of the stands to play the organ. If he'd wanted to, he even could have turned the lights on at two in the morning and shot some pucks.

Because I lived so close to the Gardens and loved being on the ice, I would often get to the rink early. Most times I walked into the Gardens in the morning, Harold's dog, T. C. Puck, would immediately start barking from the far side of the building, and I'd find myself thinking, "I wonder if Puck is going to be friendly today?" Puck was a big, 150-pound Bouvier dog that Harold loved. Puck was protective—maybe to the point of being overprotective—and he was never far from Harold's side, so if he was running over to greet me, I knew Harold wasn't far behind.

As much as he loved the organization, Harold Ballard still saw some of it as a business. After my rookie year, he got rid of Dan Maloney and hired John Brophy to take over as our new head coach. John was entirely different from Dan. John was super-intense, twenty-four-seven. It didn't matter if it was a practice, weight room training, or Game Seven of a playoff series, John did everything and anything with high intensity. That's just the way he was. He pushed us all, expecting us to rise to his challenges and follow his orders.

In training camp that year, John demanded that Kevin Maguire go out and fight any of our tough guys to prove himself. John knew Kevin was coming in to take the job as the team's heavyweight, and I was to test him. Kevin also wanted to do it, to ensure that he could make his mark and make the team. So we fought. But that wasn't enough for John. A few shifts later, Kevin came back out again, and we ended up in a big scrum. At that point, other guys jumped in because they were worried about what might happen to him if they didn't. But Kevin's job was to try to be that guy on the team, and Broph expected it. I've always said you have no friends in training camp—you can be friends with a guy after camp is over and you've both made the team.

We realized the extent of John Brophy's toughness one night when we were playing in Los Angeles. This was in the old Los Angeles Forum, which had retractable stands behind the bench, and to get past them, you either had to walk all the way around, like the players did, or you could take a shortcut underneath them. After the second period—we were losing by a few goals—he decided to cut underneath the stands, but he misjudged their height and cut his head wide open on a metal support post. John should have had stitches immediately, but he wouldn't let the trainer look at him or treat him until the end of the game. Brophy had fine, white hair, so the blood streak that was starting to form wasn't exactly hard to spot. But John insisted that we focus on the game. So, for the last twenty minutes of the game, every time we looked back at John, our eyes would be glued to the red streak colouring his white hair and dripping onto the shoulder of his sports jacket.

After the game, John finally agreed to get stitched up. That's when we realized just how resilient he was. An hour after you get cut is when stitches really start to hurt. At least, they can, unless you get the area frozen first. The doctor was getting ready to fix John up, but as he pulled out the needle, John yelled, "No freezing!" And he sat there silently as the doctor sewed up his head without anything to dull the pain. We knew then that we needed to listen to whatever John told us to do.

John's approach to the game rubbed off on us. When my second regular season with the Leafs came to a close, we had finished fourth in our division again, but with a far better record than the year before. And more important, we were back in the playoffs again.

Once again, we were matched with the top team in our division, which ended up being the St. Louis Blues. The league had changed the first-round series to a best-of-seven format starting that year, but to us, the extra games just meant more chances to get our revenge on the Blues, who had knocked us out of the playoffs the year before. We got our way, too, winning the series, four games to two. In our series-clinching game against the Blues, Brad Smith scored a goal on a breakaway that I'll never forget. We were in our end, and Smitty knocked the puck down out of the air and onto my stick before breaking out of our zone. I passed him the puck up the middle, and then Motor City Smitty took over. He blew past the other team's defence and cruised in on a breakaway, made a slick move, and buried the puck in the net. That image of Smitty celebrating—helmetless and toothless—stuck with me. Leafs fans loved him and could pick him out of a crowd anywhere after that.

We faced the Detroit Red Wings in the second round. The Red Wings had swept Chicago in the first round, so they were better rested than us. But we managed to jump out to a two-game lead in the series, and we headed back to Toronto feeling confident. Detroit took Game Three, but we answered with a win in Game Four on home ice to take a stranglehold lead of three games to one. All we needed was one more win to take us to the conference finals. But we just couldn't close it out. The Red Wings stormed back to win three straight and take the series. We were happy to see them go on to lose to the Edmonton Oilers in the next round, after which the Oilers captured their third Stanley Cup in four years.

I hated losing in the playoffs, and to have made it to the second round both years only to fall short just made me want more. I knew that my journey to a Cup was still just beginning, but I'd had a taste of what success might feel like, and I wanted more. In just two years, I'd set a team scoring record, been to the All-Star game, and taken part in two playoff runs, so I felt I was on the right track. But I knew there was more I could do, on and off the ice, to be better. I just didn't realize how far I still had to go.

Me at two years old—
my first year on skates—
at the Kelvington rink.
Courtesy of the Clark family.

Posing with my brothers Donn
(*in the blue shirt*) and Kerry
(*sitting in front*). *Courtesy of the
Clark family.*

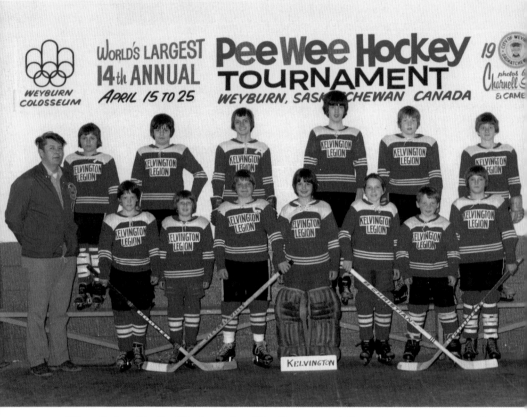

When I played in the Weyburn Pee-Wee Tournament, I was two years younger than the other kids on the team, but my size never stopped me (*first row, second from right*). Joey Kocur was our captain that year. *Courtesy of the Clark family.*

Celebrating with the Hounds after we won a Midget tournament in Swift Current (*top row, third from left*). There were plenty of other future NHLers on the team that year, including Brad Lauer, Terry Perkins, and Bob Joyce. *Courtesy of the Clark family.*

When we were having our promotional pictures taken for the 1985 World Junior tournament, I still had a black eye from a rough WHL game I'd played in just before training camp. *Courtesy of the Clark family.*

Northern Finland in December is cold, even by Saskatchewan standards. Luckily, I found this wolf-fur hat while I was there. *Courtesy of the Clark family.*

Left to right: Donn; my dad, Les; me; my mom, Alma; and Kerry. We took this photo at our cottage during one of our annual "Christmas in July" holidays. *Courtesy of the Clark family.*

Left to right: Barry Melrose, Joey Kocur, me, my brother Kerry, and Kory Kocur. *Courtesy of the Town of Kelvington.*

Standing beside Harold Ballard and Ken Spangler, the Leafs' second-round draft pick, at the 1985 NHL Entry Draft. *Colin McConnell.*

Me with my agent and good friend Don Meehan (*centre*) and Joey Kocur (*right*) at the draft. Joey had just come from a friend's barbecue to see us at the event. *Courtesy of the Clark family.*

Wherever Harold was, you were sure to find T. C. Puck, his beloved dog, right beside him. *Frank Lennon.*

Screening Rangers goalie Bob Froese in my second year in the NHL. © *Graig Abel/ Graig Abel Photography.*

In the offensive zone in the 1992–93 season, one year after I'd been named the seventeenth captain of the Maple Leafs.

A typical game in the old "Chuck" Norris Division. *Material republished with the express permission of* Toronto Sun, *a division of Postmedia Network Inc.*

Probert and I fought three times this night, the first time in nearly four years that he was able to play in Canada. *Material republished with the express permission of* Toronto Sun, *a division of Postmedia Network Inc.*

My typical pre-game routine—sitting in the stands with an ice pack on my knee, taping my stick, and collecting my thoughts. *Boris Spremo.*

Even as early as 1992, I was wearing all sorts of additional gear to help manage my injuries. *Bernard Weil.*

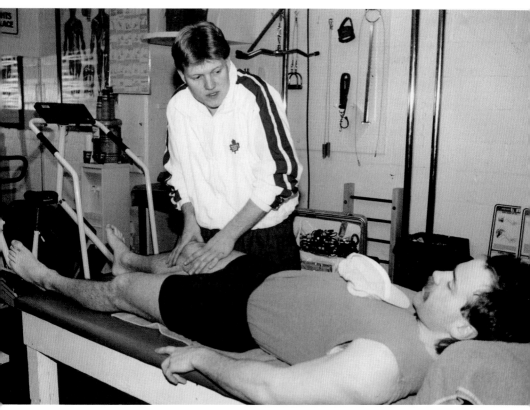

Chris Broadhurst was one of the biggest reasons why I was able to play in the NHL for as long as I did. *Colin McConnell.*

My trade to the Quebec Nordiques in 1994 marked the first time I played professionally outside of Toronto. *Denis Brodeur.*

When I was traded to Detroit I had to wear number 71, because my teammate Doug Brown was already wearing number 17.

Left to right: Kylie, Kody, and Kassie on our property in King City in 2006. This is one of my favourite photos of my kids. *Courtesy of the Clark family.*

Seeing my number raised to the rafters of the Air Canada Centre while surrounded by my family was one of the greatest experiences of my life. © *Graig Abel/Graig Abel Photography.*

5

International Play

A t the end of the 1986–87 season, I was understandably looking forward to some hard-earned downtime. But any rest I
might have had went out the window when I received an
unexpected phone call from my agent Don Meehan.

That summer, there would be another instalment of the Canada Cup, a professional international tournament. The event was
especially interesting in that era because the Soviet Union still ex-
isted, and its players weren't allowed to play professionally in North
America. Tournaments like this were the only times when the best
North Americans could face off head-to-head against the best Russians. Not only was it the biggest international competition around,
but it was held in Canada (that year, the finals would be in Montreal
and Hamilton), which meant home-ice advantage for us Canadians. The men running Team Canada that year—Glen Sather, Bobby
Clarke, and Serge Savard—had contacted Don to let him know they

wanted me to come to training camp and try out for the team. I was out in Kelvington when I got the news from Don. It was a huge honour just to be asked to try out for a team like that. Needless to say, I was pretty excited as I made my way to Montreal.

Camp was set to start in August, just two months before my twenty-first birthday. While we worked hard on the ice, the month-long training camp was one big party. We practised twice a day, but every night, we had time to ourselves. For the first part of the month, it was just us Canadians training in Montreal. But for the last two weeks of August, the American team was in town as well. All told, that meant there were more than a hundred professional hockey players living, training, and playing in Montreal for the month of August. Talk about fun.

Team Canada had brought enough players to camp so that two teams could scrimmage against each other. The NHL features the highest level of hockey in the world, and from my first game as a Leaf, I could see right away that the game was that much faster than it had been in junior. And when you narrow down the talent pool even further, to the top forty players, it ratchets up the intensity that much more. As the days went by, the roster got shorter as Coach Mike Keenan and the co–general managers cut guys to reach the twenty-three players that they needed for the tournament. We never knew when—or if—our last day at camp was coming, so I got the most I could out of skating and hanging out with these guys.

Throughout my career, I tried to learn from the guys I played with. But that camp was especially eye-opening for me. I saw first-hand just how incredibly skilled the superstars in the NHL really are. I went from summer vacation to all of a sudden playing with Wayne Gretzky, Dale Hawerchuk, and Mario Lemieux. In my time in the NHL, I had watched Gretzky passing to Jari Kurri and Bryan Trottier feeding Mike Bossy, and as I played side by side with some of those legendary players, I realized that they don't see or feel the game like the rest of us. Most people think that you pass to a player. But the great players don't do that; they pass to an area. They don't just know where you are, they know where you're going to be, and they see it happen before you do. Playing day in and day out with those guys, there were many times when the puck would suddenly appear on my stick and I would think to myself, "How did he see me?"

I was a shoot-first kind of winger. When I had the puck, I wanted to get it off my stick as fast as possible. But suddenly, I was seeing the game from the other side, and I was learning how to become a better player. Great centremen know that a talented sniper needs to be open for only a millisecond to have a chance to score. When you're in front of the net, you're never really open, because it's crowded. Defencemen are pushing you around, trying to clear the lane, and your teammates are buzzing around the net, trying to get a scoring opportunity. In those situations, less is more—as long as the blade of your stick is free, you're open. To be a good shooter is to be able to shoot in any position. Brett Hull and Joe Sakic were perfect at it.

You want to get your shot off before the goalie has a chance to think. Goalies often play the odds, and if they get square to you, you're not scoring. Even though your shot might not be hard, if the goalie has no time to react, he can't make the save. It's all about how you get it away and where you put it. And sometimes you don't have a lot of space or time to think about that. As I watched bigger players in camp, I saw how I could better use my body to create space and shield the puck in those situations, understanding that a really good centreman would know what to look for and could thread the needle, putting the puck right on my stick just so long as I gave him the opportunity.

In practice, I would get hundreds of chances to shoot and score. But in a game, I would only have something like one to five chances, and only a couple of those would be really good scoring opportunities. If I wasn't totally focused and prepared, I could easily blow a good opportunity, and I might not get another chance. Scoring is an acquired habit, just like everything else in hockey.

Paul Coffey once told me a story about one of his first practices with the Oilers. He was taking some shots on net when Glen Sather asked him, "What are you trying to do?" Coffey told Sather he was trying to go post-in from the point with his slapshot. Glen looked at him and said, "Why would you try to score like that? Why not just shoot at the middle of the net? If you miss, you'll still hit a corner. And at least all your shots hit the net."

Aiming for a corner or trying to aim a shot perfectly is great in principle. But when you're under pressure in the middle of a game, you're never going to hit the corner perfectly every time. But the net is four feet tall and six feet wide, so you can't go wrong trying to hit that larger target. After hearing that story from Paul, I started to rethink how I shot the puck. If I aimed for a corner and missed, it meant I wouldn't even hit the net. But if I aimed for the *net* and missed, I might still hit that top corner. As I worked on my shot, sometimes I would fire a puck at one of those areas of net and it would find its way to the top corner or through the five-hole, and people would congratulate me as though I'd done it on purpose, when really I was just trying to hit the net!

But no matter where you're aiming from, as a shooter, you aim from where the puck is. You don't shoot from where you're standing; you shoot from where the puck is sitting. The puck has eyes. Years of practising in my driveway and on the rinks of Kelvington had taught me to feel where that puck was in relation to my body and recognize that that's where I was shooting from. As a kid, I would practise by placing a puck on the ice and then standing behind it to see the ice from its exact point of view. I never shot from what *I* saw; I shot from what the *puck* saw. A lot of players don't understand that, when they're coming down the wing, they're not going to see a small opening by the far post from where they're looking. But the puck sees it. How many times did Mark Messier, coming down the off wing, hit that far post for a goal? He did that hundreds of times until it became one of his signature goals: far post, far side, while coming down the wing. He couldn't see that spot, but the puck could. And most goalies never stood a chance because they didn't think Messier could even see that far post to shoot at.

That's what good scorers do: they just get the puck on the net. The really great snipers, if they have time, get the puck to "areas" of the net—the far side, short side, low blocker, high glove. I liked shooting blocker side. A lot of guys tended to go above the glove, but low on the blocker side was my favourite. When I broke into the NHL, no goalie wanted to stop a shot low on the blocker side. A lot of the fun when you play goal comes from snagging a puck out of the air with your catching glove. When goalies stopped me with a move like that, I couldn't deny that it looked great. Players shoot to what they see. Because of that, a lot of goalies tended to cheat away from their glove side and show a shooter some space there. Nine times out of ten, the skater thinks they see open net by the goalie's glove, so they shoot the puck there, even though the goalie is already reading the shot and moving to make the save. Once I started to figure that this was how goalies thought, if a goalie gave me nothing on his blocker side, hoping I would shoot high glove and give him a highlight-reel save, I would instead shoot towards the short side where the goalie wasn't showing me anything. With all their body weight and their mind going to their glove side, they couldn't get back in time to stop me firing to the opposite side.

Of course, not all goalies thought this way. Dominik Hasek was the opposite of everyone else—his style wasn't one you could even teach, but it worked. And Grant Fuhr was incredibly smart, continuously watching you to see what you would do before he reacted. If you were skating in on Grant, he would come out of the net, and the second you dropped your head to shoot, he would move over six inches to whatever side you were aiming at. More than once, the puck would already be off my stick before I realized what he had done, but there was nothing I could do—my shot would hit him in the middle of the stomach and it looked awful. It wasn't rocket science—all he did was a little shuffle—but it was enough to make the save.

That was the sort of intelligence and talent that every player at that 1987 camp showed. And on top of their skill on the ice, the guys on that 1987 team were just as great off of it. Hockey teams are like any other group of people—you get the occasional bump on the log, but for the most part, the players are good people. And at that time, it was more likely than not that you all came from the same walk of life. A lot of us started out as kids growing up in small towns, and everybody remembered where they came from.

Still, we were all professional athletes, and there were lots of big personalities in the room. It takes a certain skill to handle that level and number of egos on one team, even more so if you're in an elite international setting. The coaches are constantly massaging play-ers' egos to make sure that everyone is happy, the team is clicking, and the system is working. A lot of that responsibility falls on the assistant coaches, and the way they handle that constant pressure is what sets a great assistant coach apart from an awful one. Because at some point, players are going to come off the ice and they're going to vent. A lot of times, the assistant coach knows the personalities of the players better than the head coach does. Their roles are different, and head coaches don't—or sometimes can't—spend as much time in the dressing room as the assistants do.

When I was with the Leafs, for example, if I came off the ice after the game and I needed to vent at Pat Burns, all of sudden I would find myself face-to-face with one of his assistants, Mike Kitchen or Mike Murphy, instead. Those two guys were unbelievable at their jobs; I think Kitch in particular might be one of the best ever. I could blow off steam in front of those guys and say a thousand things—most of them pretty colourful—and know that I would never get burnt for saying it. You couldn't do that directly to Burnsie—he wouldn't get it, and heated emotions might cause things to get out of hand. But Kitch and Murphy were able to pick out what I was really saying as I vented, and if any of it was useful or meaningful, they could take that part back to Pat. And if it was nothing, they could say, "He's just venting." That makes a world of difference.

Say you play like shit on a Wednesday night; you're mad at the world. So, Thursday you vent at practice. And the assistant coach recognizes that you just need to blow off steam. That means that, on Friday, you can go out and practise again with a clear mind, and suddenly you're back to normal, playing a great game on Saturday. That ability to be patient, to listen calmly, and to manage one person for the better of the team is extremely valuable, and I have a lot of respect for it.

Mike Keenan's main assistant coach with the Canada Cup team was Sather's top assistant in Edmonton in the 1980s, John Muckler. John was a great hockey guy. He understood the game, and he remembered what players liked and needed, whether they were stars, role players, or anyone else. On the Canada Cup team, he was a great buffer among what was an immensely talented group of skaters, and he made sure that everyone on that team knew their job.

That was important, because when it came to winning games, we were all business. Unfortunately, it also meant making and accepting hard decisions, and late into camp, I found out that I was being cut from the team. Since I was a late cut, I'd already dressed for a number of the exhibition games. In one of them, against the USA, I even had a pretty good tilt with Chris Nilan. Having played in the Team Canada sweater for those exhibition games, I was hoping I would be able to pull it on again for the real thing. When I found out I would have to go home instead, I was disappointed, to say the least. But, given how much talent and camaraderie you find at national camps like that, being cut from a squad like that is probably one of the few times as a player that you're not overly upset. When you look around and see guys like Cam Neely and Steve Yzerman also getting cut, it puts things in perspective.

Although I had to leave the 1987 Canada Cup team, the team never left me. I went back to Toronto to watch the games, and as I followed the Canadians throughout the tournament, it renewed my love for the sport and reminded me how incredible it can be when it's played at its finest. In my mind, Dale Hawerchuk, then the star centre for the Winnipeg Jets, was the unsung hero of that team. Hawerchuk was a guy who could—and would—do everything for his team. That's the defining quality of a great Canadian hockey player, and it's the reason he made the team. Dale was an amazingly skilled player, the sort of guy who could put up 120 points a year. But he was also good defensively, and he was smart on the ice. The Canadian team that year was stacked with talent, with guys like Wayne Gretzky, Mario Lemieux, Denis Savard, and Mark Messier all playing together. So when Hawerchuk was told that his job was to be on a third- or fourth-line checking unit, he committed to it.

For some people, putting the team first like that means that they have to swallow their pride. But when I saw how Dale so readily embraced his role and performed it the best he could, I was inspired. I realized that's what real athletes and true leaders do—they put the good of others, of the team, ahead of their personal wants. I admired that, and even better, I saw how effective it was.

The tournament was a long haul for the Canadian team. There were a lot of strong teams, and each game was a battle. But the round-robin was nothing compared to the finals. After the round-robin, Canada and the Soviet Union were first and second, respectively, and the finals were a best-of-three series. I loved that high-scoring era. Each game ended 6–5, but after every game, you could still say, "Man, Fuhr played well tonight." In the first game, Canada came from behind to tie the game, only to see the Soviet Union take it in overtime. In the second game, Canada took a 3–1 lead, only to let it slip away late in the game. With a minute left, Valeri Kamensky scored to tie the game for the Russians. With the tournament on the line for the Canadians, overtime was stressful, and one extra frame wasn't enough. Luckily, Gretzky and Lemieux connected in the second overtime to help Canada pull out a victory.

That brought the series to the deciding third game. Things didn't start off well for us, with the Soviet Union going up 3–0 early on. But Canada kept chipping away, and with just over a minute to go and the score tied 5–5, the forward line of Hawerchuk, Gretzky, and Lemieux went out to take a draw in the defensive zone. I was watching the game on TV in Toronto, and my palms were sweating as I watched them line up for the faceoff. The crowd at the game was on its feet, a mass of white shirts all cheering and waving Canadian flags. Dale won the draw, and Lemieux poked the puck past the pinching Russian defenceman. He fed the puck ahead to Gretzky, and the trio raced down the ice. Larry Murphy was streaking to the far post of the Russian goal, but Mario was trailing the play, and we all knew who was getting the puck. Gretzky dropped a pass back to Lemieux, and when he wired the puck into the top corner, the arena went crazy. As I watched the Canadian players mob each other in celebration, I was overwhelmed. I had seen the work those guys had put in, and watching it come together in such a remarkable way was a memory I would carry with me for a long time.

● ● ●

Four years later, I found myself at the Team Canada training camp again. Things were a little different this time around. For starters, the camp was held in Toronto, so I wasn't immersed in the experience the way I was in 1987. Both Dave Ellett and I were late additions. The team had needed to fill two extra spots, and as Leafs players, Dave and I were in town, so we were available on short notice.

Just like I did in 1987, I kept my eyes and ears open all through camp. One of the guys I got to know well in those short weeks was Steve Larmer. Steve was a good all-around player. He had a great set of hands, and he could pass the puck as well as he could shoot it. He knew angles and stick positions, which made him really effective in the defensive zone. He wasn't scared of anything, but he didn't go out of his way physically, because he could do everything defensively without having to throw his weight around. As I watched how Steve played the game, I hoped to learn how to give my regularly bruised body a break.

I also had the opportunity to skate with Al MacInnis every day. Al's shot was something to behold. Not only did he have one of the hardest shots I've ever seen, but it was also one of the most controlled. You don't remember Al MacInnis having his shot blocked a lot—who would want to block that cannon? But he understood what was needed in a given situation, and he tailored his play to give himself the advantage.

Every hockey player has certain skills that they can draw on. They might be able to shoot harder, skate faster, or hit more effectively than other guys. But more important than having a skill is knowing when to use it. If all you do is shoot hard all the time, you become predictable. If you skate all out nonstop, you might miss opportunities or burn yourself out. And if all you do is throw yourself into checks, then there's only so long that your body will hold up. If a player took away Al's shooting lane, he'd beat them with a slap pass down to a teammate. If the pass wasn't there and there was no shooting lane, Al could fake a move to buy time and open up space. He was a heads-up hockey player who could do it all. He knew how to use every tool in his arsenal and just when to pull each one out. It was like watching a pitcher with a lot of control of his pitches. Not only can he throw hard, but he can make it dance and do whatever he wants with it. Al was like that with his shot.

Al didn't rely on technology for his shot. The stick he played with didn't flex or jump like a golf club, as most sticks do today. Al's mechanics were perfect. If they weren't, he never would have been able to shoot the way he did. I admired Al's execution.

I loved how equipment could make my technique better, so from the beginning I'd been particular about the sticks I used. When I was a kid, I used wooden Winnwell sticks that my dad bought by the half dozen. I never liked light sticks, though—I wanted to really feel the stick in my hands. So, in my first year in the NHL, I upgraded and started using a Titan. It was a big, heavy stick, and the blade curved exactly the way I liked. That worked for a while, but I never liked the two-piece sticks because maintaining them was too much work. I used the Titan for a while until I finally settled on my favourite stick, a weighty, one-piece Bauer that I used until the end of my career.

Although the training camp in 1991 was a lot different from the one in 1987, the constant between the two was the dominance of Wayne Gretzky. Gretzky was wickedly smart, we all knew that, but watching him on the ice was completely different from watching him on a screen. He could see exactly where to put the puck at all times, and he knew how to command every situation. In one practice, my squad was playing against Gretzky's, and as he broke into the zone, he made a blind back pass that none of us saw coming. In the dressing room afterwards, I asked Gretzky why he'd made that move. To me, it had seemed risky, but he told me he was just playing the odds. "I counted four of your guys around me," he said, "and some more of my guys were in front of me. I figured that meant that another one of my guys was trailing behind me."

I couldn't argue. In the time it took most guys to figure out what play to make, Gretzky had already weighed the possibilities and computed the best possible outcome. If I had tried to read the situation and make a pass like Gretzky did, it would have been a terrible pass. But when Wayne did it, he couldn't miss—he put the puck right on the tape of his teammate's stick. Time and time again, he would make plays that had me shaking my head. But that's why he was and is called the Great One.

I had a good camp, but it still wasn't enough for me to make the team, and again, I was one of the last cuts. Sure, I was sour—I would have loved to have made the team. But my experience before the Canada Cup had taught me to be realistic when trying out for international teams. There were so many talented players that the coaches could select, and I had come to realize that, typically, when coaches and general managers were putting together a team, no player was a right or a wrong choice—it was all a matter of preference. I couldn't control the decisions that other people made. All I could do was appreciate the opportunity and make the most of it. Little did I know that there was another major opportunity heading my way.

6

Captain Crunch

After our run in the 1986–87 playoffs, the Leafs had a string of four frustrating campaigns. We never finished better than third in our division, and we made the playoffs in only two of those four seasons, losing in the first round both times. The players in the dressing room changed from year to year, but the results stayed the same; it felt like we were caught in limbo. When Harold Ballard passed away in 1990, though, the landscape changed completely. It was the end of an era.

After spending some time figuring out a new plan, the Leafs brass hired Cliff Fletcher as president and general manager on July 1, 1991. Cliff had previously been running the Calgary Flames, where he'd built the 1989 Stanley Cup–winning team, and when he arrived in Toronto, he immediately went to work rebuilding our team.

Just before I was cut from the Team Canada tryouts, Cliff called me. I thought he might want to talk about how the tryouts for the national team were going. Instead we had a very different conversation. At the end of the 1990–91 season, the Leafs' captain, Rob Ramage, had been lost to the Minnesota North Stars in an expansion draft. The team had yet to name his replacement, and Cliff told me I was going to be the new captain, the fifteenth in the team's history.

It was the greatest honour I'd received in my life. I knew that a great responsibility was being placed on my shoulders. I was only twenty-five at the time, but I felt ready for it. I had been with the Leafs for six years at that point, through some tough, lean years, and I was fired up about leading us out of that. I respected and loved the organization, and I was grateful for the chance to give back to the team and the people who had already given me so much. I had just spent time practising with and learning from some of the best players on the planet, and as I thanked Cliff, I had a clear vision in my mind of the sort of leader I had to be.

A few days before I was cut from the Team Canada roster, we had a press conference at the Hot Stove Lounge in the Gardens to announce that I was the new captain of the team. The press was all over the announcement, but as soon as the photos and interviews were over, I went directly back to the rink to continue practising with Gretzky, Messier, and Lemieux. I still remember the reception I got when I walked into the Team Canada dressing room. Everyone congratulated me and patted me on the back—just good hockey guys being happy for me.

I wasn't going to let the fact that I'd been given the C change the way I did my job. I figured that, if something changed after I put a letter on my jersey, I was getting it for the wrong reasons. As the new captain of the Leafs, I felt like my first duty was to the team and the guys around me. You can't force leadership on people. In an NHL dressing room, every guy who walks through the doors instinctively understands the dynamic. It's kind of like a wolf pack or kids on the playground. The hierarchy always emerges as people fall into their natural roles; it isn't dictated by someone from the outside. So, after the announcement, I got down to business.

When I played pickup hockey as a kid, I would sometimes see my friends do something I never understood. Instead of playing their best or trying their hardest in a game of shinny, they would sometimes hold back, as if they thought they couldn't be *too* good or else the others would turn on them for standing out. I never thought that way. I wanted to be the best I could be, no matter who I was playing, how old they were, or what level of skill they had. It was all out, every time, whether we were on the rink or the diamond. I had that drive to win, right from the beginning.

When I played sports, I *always* played to win; a victory was the end result that I aimed for. Still, I knew that winning couldn't be the be-all and end-all of my career. If I lost a game, I needed to still be able to enjoy the experience and find some measure of satisfaction in what I'd done. Some guys used stats to measure their own personal success. For me, it was more about fighting the good fight— you want to come out on top, but if you don't, then you at least want to carry yourself with some grace and dignity. I also knew that, anytime I competed, I wasn't doing it just for myself—I was competing for my team. I rarely set personal goals for myself. It is one of the main reasons I became lifelong friends with Dave Ellett. We were both similar in nature in that the team came first. We understood our jobs and what we had to contribute, but neither of us felt entitled to the spotlight. The number of goals I scored didn't really matter if we didn't win as a team.

But in the world of professional sports, those sorts of principles sometimes lose ground to the need to quantify things. The year I was named captain, I also had to negotiate a new contract, and I knew that the discussions were going to revolve around my numbers, not my past successes or my feelings about the game. When Cliff and I sat down to go over the new contract, he spelled it out for me. "I want to pay you," he said. "But if you're only playing twenty games a year, I'm going to take the heat for paying you big bucks if you're not showing anything for it because you're injured all the time."

Although I'd been in the league only a few years, I was getting injured frequently. Between 1987–88 and 1989–90, I played only eighty-one regular-season games—one year's worth of hockey in three seasons. Even though I was now the captain, to the owners I was still a potential liability—they didn't know what level I would perform at, and they weren't willing to take a risk and sign me for the long haul because there were too many unknowns. To compromise, Cliff set targets for me for games played, points, and goals. I would receive small bonuses if I played forty-five games, fifty-five games, sixty-five games, and eighty games, with similar incentives if I scored twenty, twenty-five, thirty, thirty-five, forty, forty-five, and fifty goals. It was on me to earn the money. As Cliff said, "I want to pay you like you're a forty-goal guy; but for me to do that, you have to actually score forty goals." I understood what Cliff was doing and I wasn't worried about it. My drive to succeed—to be the best, to win—was a strong one, and I liked to earn my keep.

Cliff Fletcher played a major role in my career. He was the man who rebuilt the Leafs into one of the best teams in the NHL in the early 1990s, and the magic of my seasons as the Leafs' captain would have never happened if he hadn't been hired. After naming me captain and locking down my contract, he wasted no time in improving the team. He went on to make a lot of big moves in 1991–92, the most memorable ones being the trades that brought us Doug Gilmour and Grant Fuhr. Then, after the 1991–92 season, he hired Pat Burns as the new head coach of the Leafs. There's no question that Burnsie's arrival, and the new template he created, were what really put us on the path to being winners.

The transformation wouldn't be painless. We learned early in Burnsie's reign that, as a team, we were going to have to play the way *he* wanted us to play. And the learning curve would be steep. His system was a form of the trap, and he set out detailed rules about what he expected us to do in all three zones of the ice. For the system to work, everybody on the team had to be on the same page.

Burnsie's way of making that happen was through constant repetition in practice. And Pat Burns's practices lasted two hours a day. There was nobody tougher on his players than Burnsie, and some things got you immediately blacklisted. Turning the puck over in the neutral zone was a cardinal sin. If you turned the puck over in the neutral zone, you were benched. But if everybody accepted the assignment that Burns set out for them, the system worked great. We struggled with it until Christmas, but eventually, everything clicked as each guy on the team bought into his role. That was when we finally felt like a team.

It took us a couple of months to absorb Pat's system to the point that everybody could follow it without thinking. After that, what we did on the ice was instinctive—no more pausing to think through your decision beforehand. Because if you have to think through a decision during a game, chances are you'll get beat. When you're playing at the highest level, there is no time to think. Getting a team to the point where everyone can perform that way is immensely difficult. Through blood, sweat, and swears, Burnsie got us there. He had a self-assurance—some might call it an arrogance—that gave us an identity. He had confidence in himself, his system, and his team.

Each coach has a different style and skill set. If a coach was a fake and couldn't sell us his system, we could see right through him. But that never happened with Pat Burns. He forced you to believe in his methods. Pat pushed a lot of buttons. He had been a tough cop before he became a coach, and he wasn't there to be the nice guy. A lot of times, he actually wanted the whole team to hate him, and he had two main tools to make that happen—his stare and his yell. Pat had the same bark, regardless of what mood he was in. So when he yelled at you to come and see him in his office, you didn't know what you were in for until you walked into the room. A lot of the time, though, Pat didn't have to say anything to let us know he was pissed off. He would just stare us down. Sometimes, his assistant coaches, Mike Kitchen and Mike Murphy, got the evil eye, too. Even Doug Gilmour—our star player, who was usually better than anyone on the ice—would occasionally face Burns's searing glare.

Pat was definitely a tough-love, old-school kind of coach. We saw some of his lighter side during the summer, when the stress of the season wasn't weighing on him. I ran into Pat a number of times after I was done playing, and our relationship was better after the fact than it was when I was playing. We'd been through wars together, and when you walk through fire with a guy, you can look back on your time together in a better light.

Everything Burnsie did—the mind games, the displays of temper, the attitude—was meant to pull our team together. That's what made the guys on that Leafs team of the early nineties such a great group. Everybody respected each other, understood their role, and we all stood together. If someone was in Burnsie's doghouse, the team would rally together to protect that guy. Nothing was said, but whoever it was that got called out would understand that we all had his back. Because we all knew that a loss wasn't the fault of any one person—we won and lost as a team. True closeness on a hockey team isn't something that people suddenly decide to create. It happens by itself and builds over time.

At first, I didn't understand what Burns was doing. When you're right in the middle of it with someone in a position of authority like that, your first thought is often that the guy is just a prick. But later on, I was able to look back and understand why he had done the things he did. Thinking about the way he pushed our buttons, it hit me: he understood that the harder he pushed us, the more we would have each other's backs and watch out for one another.

That's when I got it. My job wasn't to fight Burns's methods. Everyone, from the players to the PR reps to the maintenance staff, understood that Burns was in charge. Some days it was my job to be the whipping boy and take the heat from him. Other nights that fell on other guys, and my role was to help support that other guy.

Luckily, there was a lot of depth and character on those teams Burns coached. We had guys like Dougie and Mike Foligno, who had incredible leadership skills. That's what makes a team. One guy can never do it all himself. He needs a group of solid leaders around him. And on those teams in the early nineties, we had exactly that in our dressing room.

Cliff and Burnsie both came into Toronto with a self-assurance that spread through the team. The way they carried themselves was a model for us—it made us want to be better players. And that confidence was something we desperately needed playing in Toronto. To play hockey with the Leafs, you need to have confident people who have made it through difficult times. They're the ones who know what it takes to win. True leaders have an inner confidence to face down everyone who tells them they're wrong and say, "No. I'm going to keep doing it my way because I believe it's the right way." And when that doesn't work anymore, the best leaders will also have the ability to listen to coaches, teammates, or friends, who help to steer them in a new direction.

● ● ●

My role on the Leafs changed as I developed under Burnsie's tenure. I was starting to mature and learn what was expected of me not just as a player, but as a leader. On the ice, that meant I wasn't fighting as much or running around trying to hit everything. Pat was the coach who taught me that I didn't have to do it all in a single shift. Not every game was going to require me to do every single thing it takes to win—fighting, scoring, hustling, passing, blocking, checking. Burnsie reinforced the lesson that the better the team is, the easier it is for each person on the team to play the game. If everybody is doing his job, then nobody should be burned out at the end of a game. That allows you not only to play better from game to game, but to extend your career, too, because you can focus on improving at your job.

I'd never thought about it that way. I had been so focused on doing everything I could, every single moment, that I never stopped to consider how that might be affecting the team or my future. To me, success meant doing more—harder shots, heavier hits, and faster feet. Burnsie showed me that sometimes you get the best results by doing less, just so long as you do things better. By the early nineties, our team had become so good that I was finally able to scale it back. I had a solid sense of confidence every time I stepped on the ice, and it made me a better player.

I had a good reason to be confident, too—we had a darn good team. I loved the playoffs in 1993 and 1994, because the postseason was one of the few times I got to play with Doug Gilmour. Of course, a lot of the time, that was only because Burnsie had Dougie centering two lines—one with Dave Andreychuk and Nik Borschevsky, and another with myself, Glenn Anderson, or Rob Pearson.

Although Burns's system was strict in a lot of ways, there was one exception: Doug Gilmour. If you were on a line with Dougie, you had a green light, because that was the offensive line and you were supposed to create whatever chances you could. There's no question that Dougie was our superstar back then—he was the guy who was creating the offence. By the end of the playoffs, Doug's weight had dropped to 165 pounds thanks to sheer exhaustion. He was pale and gaunt, but still he was unbelievable. In my mind, Dougie so excelled at every facet in the game that he was the best player in the NHL in that two-year window.

Not only was Gilmour our best player on the ice, but he was also a master of keeping us loose. And he was so unassuming—he played a lot of practical jokes on me that got blamed on somebody else. Doug loved putting tiny holes in the bottom of the Styrofoam coffee cups we had in the dressing room. He would come in early, take the whole stack of cups, and poke holes in a few of them. Nobody could tell they were there . . . until the coffee was in the cup. Once the coffee hit the Styrofoam and it heated up, the hole got larger and the coffee would start to spill out of the bottom. Now, Doug would have set this up a week earlier, so nobody would ever think to blame it on him, and he was patient enough to bide his time until a coach or a teammate finally picked up one of those cups.

That didn't mean he always got away scot-free, though. I endured a lot of pain in my hockey career, but there was one sort of discomfort that I couldn't stand: I hated going to the dentist because I hated the mouth pain so much. Luckily for me, I never lost a single tooth playing hockey. But Dougie wasn't so fortunate. While we were teammates, he decided to get his teeth fixed. He'd lost a number of them over the years, and he had a set of dentures that he would wear when he wasn't on the ice. But one day, Doug decided to finally have the bridgework done and get four new teeth put in permanently. The very first game after Dougie got his teeth fixed, we were playing the Blackhawks, and during the game, he got tripped up. As he was falling to the ice, he got hit in the face with a stick, and all four of his brand-new teeth were knocked out. So back Dougie went to the dentist. It was at that point that Doug decided to wait until after he retired from the NHL to get permanent dental work done again.

Having guys like Dougie in the dressing room was important, because we needed to be able to let off steam. We couldn't be dead serious all the time, and we had to be "on" so much when we were away from the rink anyway. In Toronto, you're a Leaf twenty-four hours a day, seven days a week. So you needed to have a sense of normalcy within the dressing room and have fun with the guys— you couldn't cave to the pressure. As a player, the only people you can trust are in that room. You're all in the same shit, whether you're winning or losing. You all understand it, and you either get through it together or not at all. Every team will face challenges that are unique to its time and situation, but the general pressures are the same. You couldn't be poking each other's eyes out just because of how long a losing streak was.

Playing on a losing or slumping team is difficult. You're anxious to change the tempo of the game any way you can, and you're constantly playing catch-up. When you're losing during a home game, you'll do anything you can to get the crowd into the game and on your side and energize the team. When you're down two goals, you might try to fight someone to get your team started again. If you're on a team that is constantly losing by a goal early or that constantly finds itself down by two goals, then power forwards like me end up going out of their way to wake the team up or get something going physically. And that style of play is way more demanding on the body. But when you're winning, you don't want that. When you're up, you're thinking, "Hey, we're up, let's not start anything." To keep ourselves in that positive state of mind, we treated the dressing room as our safe zone, our sanctuary, the one spot where nobody could get to us.

With Burnsie's system in place and talented players like Gilmour on the ice, we were turning the team around. But something was still missing. When the 1992–93 season started, Grant Fuhr was our starting goalie. Grant was as confident a player as I ever played with. If the score was tied heading into the third period, Grant never failed to tell us, "If you guys score, we win." He was good enough to back up his words, and he was so convincing, we all believed him. We just had to put one in, and we knew that Grant would stand on his head to get us the win.

But in February 1993, the team traded Grant to Buffalo for Dave Andreychuk. We were surprised, given how well he'd been playing. But then we were introduced to the man who had been tapped to take Grant's place and who became the third key to our playoff success in 1993 and 1994: Felix Potvin. Felix came up from the Leafs farm team in St. John's, Newfoundland, and from his first game, we could see that he was an incredibly talented goalie. But he had a very different personality from most other keepers. Where a lot of goalies were brash or had colourful personalities, Felix was a quiet, self-confident young man who joined the team as a twenty-one-year-old, but who played like he was ten years older than he was. Like all good players, Felix trusted himself and his abilities. We all liked him right away.

Potvin's job was harder than just about anyone else's, and he rose to the challenge. We never worried about Felix, because he was good in every game. We would be in a tight, 1–1 game and Felix would stop a two-on-one rush or a breakaway to hold down the fort. Seeing him pull off saves like that would give us a major boost, and the momentum change would see us turn the tables and score a goal or two to steal the win. People would see that we won 3–1 and think the offence was clicking, when really it was Felix's defence that held us together until the scorers could get going. We could trust that he would make key save after key save whenever we needed it. And in front of him were six defencemen—Dave Ellett, Todd Gill, Jamie Macoun, Bob Rouse, Dmitri Mironov, and Sylvain Lefebvre—who formed as good a group as any you could find.

With all the pieces in place, we were ready to make a run in the 1993 playoffs.

We'd had a good season, but not an outstanding one. We finished third in our division, and that meant that we would face second-place Detroit in the opening round of the playoffs. The Red Wings had finished just ahead of us in the standings and had a solid team, and Toronto hadn't beaten Detroit in the playoffs since 1964, so the media didn't peg us as serious contenders. But the next few weeks would show how a group of players that seems only average in the regular season can take its game to the next level when the season is on the line.

When I look back on my career, I don't miss training camp, and I don't miss the grind that goes with the regular season. But I do miss the playoffs. On any given night in the postseason, your entire season is on the line, and there's an incredible energy in each city for every single game. At the end of the day, sports is about winning, and the playoffs are when that all comes to a head. They were the realization of everything I had dreamed about as a kid and all the work I put in during the regular season.

But as exciting as a postseason run can be for a professional athlete, reality still sets in. The playoffs come after eight months of grueling regular-season play, when you're not just playing a game every other night, you're travelling, practising, and staying in condition, too. It's a grind. That's why you need twenty players, and that's why you build a lineup of different kinds of athletes. The regular season is a grind, a war of attrition. It takes a toll.

Leading up to the 1993 playoffs, I noticed that my body was needing more time to warm up and I was spending increasing amounts of time doing rehab with Leafs athletic therapist Chris Broadhurst just to get ready to play. But no matter what I was going through to get ready to play, I never took games off. I wanted nothing more than to be out on the ice. I never got to the point where I said, "Coach, I'm not playing tonight." I never had an issue with playing hurt.

But once the playoffs come around, things change. You play every other day, and if you're an average winger, you play fifteen minutes per game. If you're especially busy as a forward, you might play twenty minutes or so, and a big-minute defenceman might play somewhere closer to twenty-eight. So every game day, I would tell myself, "I have fifteen minutes of work every forty-eight hours." Of course, that doesn't include preparation and travel time. But what it all boils down to is those fifteen minutes. I have a sore shoulder? My back is flaring up? Doesn't matter. I never felt 100 percent in my first shift of a game. But after a few minutes, I would get into a nice rhythm. Before I knew it, the first period would be over, and that's when I knew I had made it. No matter how much I was hurting, I would will myself through this first five minutes of every first period until I was able to block out any pain I was feeling.

I wanted to play, but sometimes the thought of the pain I was about to face would give me pause. So I started to simplify the game in my mind, convincing myself that I could get through anything. I broke it down one period, one minute, one shift at a time. Fifteen minutes. Thirty shifts. Forty-second intervals. I began to reduce the game to its most basic parts to make it bearable. Afterwards, I would allow myself to deal with whatever hurts and injuries I might have. But in the heat of the game, I would eliminate everything else going on around me. Playing in a loud arena helped. I could feel the energy in those buildings and the noise that the crowd would make, even before the puck dropped. The hype and action that surround a hockey game—especially at playoff time—are the reasons we all loved the game as kids. We didn't play the game so that we could play in a silent arena in a game that doesn't mean anything. I wanted the stakes to be high, the pressure to be on, and the game to be on the line.

During the playoffs, my game-day routine was the same as it was during the regular season, with just one exception. Before each playoff game, I would take my sticks into the stands. I would sit there with Harry Neale and Bob Cole from *Hockey Night in Canada* nearby, tape my sticks, and visualize the game. I'd imagine who I was playing against, how I would move and react on the ice, and try to get my mind ready for what was coming that night.

Our opening-round series against Detroit hit all the marks. It was crazy from beginning to end. We lost the first two games big-time, 6–3 and 6–2, and it looked like the predictions about us were going to come true. We went back to Toronto for Game Three with our tails between our legs. Those were rough days. Not only had we lost the first two games of the series, but I was getting killed in the press. I was practising a couple of hours a day, but after that, I had nothing but time, so I read everything that was being written about me. The Toronto media was roasting me daily, and the papers were calling me everything and anything you could imagine. Some of the local writers really went after me. They said I wasn't living up to my potential, that I wasn't scoring enough, that I wasn't a real leader. And just about every single one called me out for not fighting Bob Probert. In their minds, I wasn't doing anything to change the momentum of the games; I wasn't a true competitor.

I tried to block out the noise, but it was all around me. I knew that I had to step up my game and that Game Three would be a pivotal moment in the series. And I tried not to be bitter about what was being said about me. Because what the reporters didn't know was that, before Game One, Burnsie had outlined a game plan that was ironclad. He told me straight out, "You will *not* fight Probert, ever, in this series." He didn't want me fighting Probert because it would only fire up the Detroit crowd. It was a strategic decision. And as the captain, I knew I had to follow orders. But as a competitor, I just wanted to let out my frustration and find some way of getting us back into the series.

I was determined to silence the critics in Game Three. We stormed out of the gate, taking a two-goal lead in the first seven and a half minutes, and we won 4–2. Early in the third, I scored a power play goal that proved to be the game winner, and assisted on Rob Pearson's insurance goal. That set us up for a 3–2 win in Game Four that evened the series at two games apiece. We were amped as we headed back to Detroit for Game Five. The matchup that night was intense, as the game went back and forth, but we quieted the crowd at Joe Louis Arena with a 5–4 overtime win that put us one win away from taking the series. Given the criticism I had been facing, I was glad that I had done my part, scoring the tying goal halfway through the third period and then assisting on Foligno's game winner. Game Six would be back in Toronto, too, and I thought about how sweet it would be to win the series in front of the Gardens crowd, showing everyone who had doubted us that we had what it took to win.

I didn't get my wish, though. The Red Wings dominated the game, rolling over us and winning, 7–3, powered by five straight goals in the second period that obliterated the 2–1 lead we'd taken in to the first intermission. All the energy and excitement that built up as a result of our three wins suddenly seemed to fade away, and as we sat in the dressing room after the game, thinking about the trip back to Detroit, we needed something to get us going. Burnsie walked into the dressing room, stood quietly in front of us for a minute, and then said, "I don't give a shit what you guys do tonight or tomorrow. Just make sure you're ready to play Game Seven!"

I took Burnsie's words literally. I travelled with the team to Detroit, and then I did nothing until game time. I didn't participate in the morning skate, I didn't speak with the media, and I didn't work out. I did nothing but rest and relax. I did some rehab with Chris Broadhurst, but my goal was to stay off the ice until game time.

When I finally arrived at the arena for the pregame warm-up, Burns chirped me and asked, "How come you weren't at the pregame skate?"

"You told us that you don't care, just as long as you come ready to play Game Seven," I replied. "And I'm ready to play."

Burnsie looked at me and could only say, "Okay." He ate his words and walked away.

Neither we nor Detroit gave any quarter that game. We went back and forth, trading leads. I assisted on a couple of goals as we threw everything we could at the Red Wings. Three periods weren't enough to settle the game, though. And that meant overtime in Game Seven in the enemy's house—it was everything I'd ever wanted.

Two minutes into the extra frame, Dougie took a draw in the Detroit zone. The next minute felt like one of the longest I'd ever spent on the ice. We were buzzing through the Red Wings' zone, cycling the puck and firing over and over at their goalie, Tim Cheveldae. Every time the Red Wings tried to clear the puck, we'd be right there, checking and harassing them to knock the puck free. When they finally did clear their zone, we fired the puck right back in. The puck rolled along the boards, and I beat the Red Wings' defenceman to it on the left wing. I made a quick pass back to Dougie at the top of the circle, and then I barreled towards the net. Dougie saw Bob Rouse stepping in off the right point, and he teed up a shot for him. I was standing by the left post as I watched Bob fire the puck hard and low. To my right, Nik Borschevsky had positioned himself perfectly, right between the hash marks. As Bob got his shot off, I thought to myself that if Nik didn't get a stick on the puck, I'd be able to tip it in. But there was no need. Nik deflected Bob's shot perfectly around Cheveldae, and the puck flew into the net in front of me.

Our bench launched into a frenzy. The trainers sprayed water bottles in the air and we tossed sticks and gloves aside as we piled together in celebration. We weren't supposed to win that game or that series, and the rush that we felt after Nik's goal was unlike anything I'd ever experienced.

We didn't have any time to rest on our laurels, though. Just two days later, we were in St. Louis to kick off our second round. It was another war of attrition. For seven games, we peppered Curtis Joseph with shots, and each and every time, he stood up to the test. In Game One alone, we took forty-two shots on Cujo in regulation time, but we could only score one goal. When we came out flying, we felt great—we assumed it was only a matter of time before our shots started going in. But as the game went on and Cujo continued to stand up to us, facing another twenty-one shots in overtime, our bench became incredibly tense. The way he was playing, we knew that the Blues only needed one chance to steal a game from us. We couldn't afford to make any mistakes, but still, it took some late-game heroics for us to come out on top.

The game went to double overtime, and at this point, we didn't know what we could do to beat Cujo. Two and a half minutes into the second extra period, I was on the bench as Dougie took a draw in our end. He won the faceoff cleanly, and Todd Gill moved the puck down the ice. For the next minute, their line cycled the puck through the Blues' zone, chasing and pinching to keep St. Louis penned in. Eventually, Dougie found himself behind the St. Louis net with the puck on his stick. We watched from the bench as Dougie patiently waited, looking for an opening. We didn't know what he was going to do, and it looked like he had nowhere to go. He started to walk up the left side of the net before quickly cutting back down behind it. Cujo and the Blues' defenceman Bret Hedican both bought the trick and immediately jumped over to cover the right side of the net, expecting Dougie to try a wraparound. But as they slid over, Dougie whipped around and brought the puck back up the left side on his backhand. As Cujo dove desperately back and threw his stick out from the far post, Dougie slipped the puck underneath his hands to win the game.

Game Two was a similar story. We launched another forty-eight shots at Joseph in regulation time—twenty-three of them in the first period—and again we could only get one past him. The game also dragged on to double overtime, but this time Cujo remained unbeatable, making ten more saves, and the Blues came away with a 2–1 win that tied the series. We traded wins with the Blues over the next four games, and to his credit, Felix Potvin was outstanding for us every night. But it wasn't until Game Seven that we were finally able to crack Cujo. He'd been unbelievable, but night after night of exhausting work took its toll, and both he and the Blues had run out of gas. We pounded them, 6–0, in front of a home crowd at the Gardens. My shot was really clicking that night, and I scored a couple of goals. Late in the game, I was coming into the Blues' zone on a two-on-one, and instead of passing, I took a slapshot that nailed Cujo in the head, sending his mask flying. I felt a little bad—I definitely wasn't aiming for his head. But as we waited for the trainers to get Cujo a replacement helmet, it did feel good to know that we'd finally found our scoring touch again and that we'd kept our season alive.

But even with everything we'd accomplished in those first two series, they were just a warm-up for what came next. A couple of days after we finished off the Blues, Wayne Gretzky and the Los Angeles Kings rolled into town to face us. That Kings team was phenomenal. At the time, people underestimated them because they were so young. But with players like Gretzky up front and Rob Blake on the blue line, they were serious competition, and they were ready to prove it.

The Kings sent us a message in the very first game of the series. Dougie had just carried the puck over the Kings' blue line and dumped it into their corner. As he cut across the top of the circle, Marty McSorley stepped up and demolished him. No one had ever taken a run at Gilmour before, and it looked like McSorley was aiming directly for his head—it was a huge check, and Dougie stayed down after he hit the ice. I saw red, and I knew that I had to answer the bell and stick up for our best player. So I immediately raced over to McSorley and we got into in a wild fight. This wasn't a strategic fight. My blood was pounding. McSorley and I stood there, raining rights down on each other's heads. I didn't try to position him or circle him around—I was just pumping my fist back and forth as fast as I could. Marty had used the hit to try to tell us that the Kings were coming after each and every one of us—even our skilled players, like Gilmour. And I was responding that if they tried anything, they'd be punished for it. At moments like this, rivalries are built.

After the game, I was sitting in the dressing room and talking to Dave Ellett, trying to make sense of what had happened. We relived the hit, the fight, and how the two coaches, Pat Burns and Barry Melrose, had almost gotten into it between the benches. While they never did come to blows, the fans in the Gardens went insane when they saw Burnsie try to cross the benches to get at Melrose. By that time, there was complete mayhem on the ice and in the stands. Kelly Hrudey, the Kings' goalie, had to take cover in his net at one point so that he wouldn't get hit by the garbage that fans were throwing on the ice. That whole scene set the tone for the series. As Dave and I talked, we wondered what the next few games would bring and what we'd have to do to keep the Kings in check. At one point, I wondered if it would have been smarter for me to go after Gretzky—since Mc-Sorley had gone after our best player, maybe I should've gone after theirs.

I didn't like that sort of retaliation, though. When people talk about a code in hockey, I say my only code was to win. That's why I played the game in the first place: to win. That meant winning every shift, every encounter, and every game. A hockey game is a series of small individual battles. Nasty little one-on-ones and two-on-twos. Yes, it is a team game. But it's a team game that's won through those head-to-head confrontations. It all comes down to who will win the battle for the five feet of ice you want to occupy. I picked my fight with McSorley that night, and I knew we would have more struggles to come, because like me, Marty battled for every inch of space on the ice that he could get.

Incredibly, all of this was happening before we'd even reached the second game of the series. From that point on, the atmosphere was even more electric in the Gardens, if that was possible. During the games, the arena would get so charged and full of energy that the heat would ratchet up to 25 to 30 degrees Celsius. Most guys hated when the Gardens got that warm, but I loved it. I felt better sweating than I did freezing; I'd spent enough time playing in icy barns, and I didn't need to go back. So I loved the fact that things were heating up in every sense.

We took Game One, 4–1, after which the Kings won the second and third games of the series. We tied things up when we won Game Four in Los Angeles. We went back to the Gardens for Game Five, and we took a stranglehold on the series when we won, 3–2, in over-time. As we flew down to Southern California once more, we felt so close to the Stanley Cup final that we could taste it. Montreal had won its series against the New York Islanders a few days earlier, so we knew the Canadiens were watching our series closely to see who they'd be playing for the ultimate prize. I tried to focus on the game in front of me, but I couldn't fully let go of the thought that we had a chance to beat the Kings on their home ice and set ourselves up for an all-Canadian Stanley Cup showdown.

As we got ready on the day of Game Six, though, something was off. As we started our pregame warm-up, my back started to act up. I figured it was just the wear and tear from all the games and travel in the playoffs that year, so I tried to skate through the discomfort and keep loosening up. I had already spent most of the day receiving therapy from our trainers, but the pain just got worse and worse. But I quickly realized I was better off getting rehab than skating around. So I went back into the dressing room for more work with Chris.

At that point in the playoffs, I had general overall body soreness. Had it been a regular-season game, I wouldn't have played; I would have rested to avoid risking an injury. But there was no way I was sitting out that night.

When the game started, I could barely move around the ice. Every movement, I was in agony. And yet, somehow, the puck kept following me around all game. Every time I swung my legs over the boards and stepped on the ice, my back would flare up and I'd wonder if I could go another shift. But then the puck would appear on my stick and my old instincts would take over, taking my mind off the pain. We were facing an uphill battle, though. We went up 1–0 less than a minute into the game, but the Kings tied it up midway through the first period. Four minutes into the second, when I scored a goal to put us ahead, 2–1, I felt like the game was ours for the taking. The rest of the guys felt the same way, too. Every time we scored, we celebrated a little more intensely, and every goal sparked a new fire in us.

But the memory of those early goals quickly faded when the Kings scored three times on the power play to take a 4–2 lead into the second intermission. Suddenly, a game that had been ours for the taking seemed almost out of reach. But I wasn't ready to give up. The thought of a Stanley Cup final had me fired up, and as we went into the third period, I set aside all the pain and discomfort I'd been feeling and told myself I had to do whatever it took to get the job done. That attitude paid off when I scored my second goal of the game in the third period, bringing us within one. Everyone on the team was digging deep as we did everything we could to close the gap, but in the dying minutes of the game, we were still down by a goal. I was on the bench when Burnsie came over to me, tapped me on the shoulder, and said, "Clarkie, if we get the puck in the right spot in the offensive zone, Felix is coming off and you're going out." That meant I had one job: put the puck in the net.

With just over a minute to go in the game, the Kings carried the puck into our zone and Potvin made a great stop on the odd-man rush. He knew we didn't have any time to waste, so rather than freezing the puck for a faceoff, he skated the puck out of his crease and knocked it up the ice. We got the puck deep into the Kings' zone, and as we set up in their corner, Burns started yelling to Potvin to come to the bench. I leapt over the boards and raced to catch up with the play. As I crossed the Kings' blue line, Dougie had the puck in the opposite corner. The L.A. defencemen were all focused on Dougie and the puck down low, leaving me clear in the high slot. Dougie waited as long as possible, and then sent a pass through the traffic in front of the net, a perfect tape-to-tape feed. I took one step, and then I unleashed a wrist shot into the top corner, tying the game.

Our bench went wild. Guys were jumping up and down, pumping their arms in the air. The Kings fans were stunned—their team had looked like it was on the brink of guaranteeing Game Seven, and suddenly we were heading to overtime, where anything can happen.

Unfortunately for us, that proved to be all too true. Just over a minute into the extra frame, we were killing a penalty when the Kings got the puck to Gretzky at the top of the circle. Gretzky took a slapshot, but one of our defencemen, Jamie Macoun, got in front of it. The puck bounced off Macoun's skates towards Dougie, who went to clear the puck. Gretzky skated up behind Dougie and tried to take the puck off of him, but missed Doug's stick, and as he followed through, the blade of his stick cut Dougie's face open. We saw it happen from the bench and we were immediately on our feet, expecting a high-sticking penalty to be called against Gretzky. After we'd just killed off a penalty of our own, we were desperate for the return call that would let us swing the momentum in our favour. But it never came. Referee Kerry Fraser talked to his linesmen right after the high stick, but we could tell from his body language that he wasn't going to call the penalty. As the captain, it was on me to confront Kerry about the call. But as I argued with him, I knew that there would be no changing his mind. That season, a high-sticking penalty that drew blood didn't just mean a penalty—it meant an immediate ejection from the game. And there was no way the ref was going to kick Gretzky out.

They'd penalized Glenn Anderson with thirteen seconds left in the third period. Nobody had been hurt on the foul he got called for. If the refs hadn't made that call, we wouldn't have started overtime in a shorthanded situation. The missed call against Gretzky just added insult to injury.

When we realized the call wouldn't be overturned, as pissed off as we were, there was nothing we could do about it. The game wasn't over, and we still had a chance to win. We tried to regain our rhythm and focus, but we weren't able to recover. A few seconds after the high stick against Dougie, Luc Robitaille fed a pass out to Gretzky, who buried the puck and won the game for Los Angeles, 5–4. Despite our best efforts, we were headed back to Toronto for Game Seven.

The final game of the series was our twenty-first in forty-one nights, and we were a bruised and battered bunch. But we refused to give up. The Kings took a 2–0 lead in the first period, but we came back to tie it in the second before they scored to make it 3–2. We again drew even early in the third, but L.A. scored twice in thirty-seven seconds to make it 5–3 with a little over three minutes to play. Still, we battled. Dave Ellett scored with 1:07 left in the third, but that was all we had left. Gretzky had all the magic that night, with three goals and an assist, and when the game ended with Los Angeles winning, 5–4, our season was over. It was the most disappointing loss I could imagine.

In the playoffs, all you want is a chance to win. Personal glory doesn't come into it. In most games, a hat trick is something to celebrate. But we'd lost Game Six, so in the big picture, it wasn't important. Had we taken that game in Los Angeles, we would have won the series and faced the Montreal Canadiens in Toronto's first Stanley Cup final appearance since 1967, and not being able to get there felt so much worse because, deep down, we believed we had what it took to beat the Canadiens. What an experience that would have been. It could have been a great story, but instead our season ended with us falling just short. Our only consolation was that we'd had a taste of winning, and we knew we'd be back.

● ● ●

In the fall of 1993, our training camp was held in London, England. Because of the travel, the team only brought twenty-eight players, and it was easily the best camp ever, because it wasn't traditional. We were practising and playing, of course, but we were also travelling and getting to know each other. And because of the long postseason run we'd had the year before and the fact that we were travelling while training, Burnsie backed off a bit in his practices. Usually, his skates were tough, but that year they were more enjoyable than they'd ever been.

It proved to be the right approach, because we raced out of the gate at the start of the season, winning our first ten games in a streak that lasted three weeks. There were maybe four games in that stretch that we should have lost but we just happened to win by getting the right bounces. At the time, we didn't care *how* we were winning—we just loved that it was happening. But Burnsie knew we didn't deserve to win all of those games.

In one game early that season, I was a little late on my back check, and as I tried to get back to our end, we got scored on. After the goal, I skated by Dave Ellett and said, "I'm sorry, that was my guy." Ellett looked at me and said, "Yeah, well they're booing at me and not you! And make sure to tell Burnsie you were late on the back check, because he's going to blame me for the goal!" I chuckled as I skated away—I knew Dave well enough to recognize that he wasn't that mad at me, and we both knew how competitive Burnsie was. Mistakes like that meant that, even during our winning streak, we would still have two-hour practices because Burnsie was pissed at how poorly we were playing. It was only when we started to lose some games that he gave us days off.

That fast start was huge for us that season. After sweeping our first ten games, we were more like a .500 hockey team the rest of the year. Had it not been for the streak, we wouldn't have made the playoffs. But we did make it to the postseason that year, and as soon as we were there, we got hot again. The memory of losing to the Kings the year before was still fresh in our minds, and we wanted a shot at redemption. There's nothing to get your competitive spirit raging like wanting to make up for a painful loss.

Our first series was against Ed Belfour and the Chicago Blackhawks. I knew how good a goaltender Eddie Belfour was, and how intense a competitor he was, but I also knew that you could get in his kitchen. In the playoffs, every little action and thought matters—anything you can do to throw off the other team helps. Goalies are very territorial by nature. You mess with what they see as their zone, or the area they want to be in, and they will lash out. I liked messing with goalies in this way, but Eddie was a guy who didn't take kindly to that kind of thing.

It was Game Two of the series and we were tied 0–0 in overtime. I was just outside of Eddie's crease, and the puck had come back to Todd Gill at the point. Just as Todd shot the puck, I gave Eddie a little tap on his stick—nothing major, just a little "love tap," but it was enough to distract Eddie, and the puck went past him for the winning goal. All of a sudden, we had a 2–0 series lead.

Eddie lost it. He skated after referee Bill McCreary, complaining that I had been in his crease and had banged his stick. Bill consulted the video-replay officials upstairs, but they had no problem with what I had done, so the goal stood. As I walked off the ice, Burnsie asked me what Eddie was complaining about. When I told him, he just shook his head and said, "Well, the game's over. We won."

We ended up beating the Blackhawks in the first round of the playoffs in six games. I picked up an assist in Game Five as we won, 1–0. Then Mike Gartner scored the game winner in Game Six, another 1–0 victory, to seal the series victory for us. Up next were the San Jose Sharks. They had the last seed in the playoffs that year, but they were a tough opponent. Our series went to seven games, and we had to win the last two games back to back to clinch it. I scored two goals in Game Six—a 3–2 overtime victory—and then I had two goals and an assist in Game Seven as we beat San Jose, 4–2, to win the series. That meant that we were heading back to the conference finals for a second straight year.

One of the things I will never forget about our run in the 1994 playoffs was how tough Dougie was throughout it all. He broke his ankle in the first game of the opening-round series against Chicago, but it didn't keep him out of a single game. For the rest of the playoffs, he was getting that ankle frozen every night. It was excruciating to watch as he went into the trainer's office to get five or six needles so he wouldn't feel any pain. On some nights, the pain was so bad that he had to numb his foot to the point that he couldn't even feel his skate. Doing that for a single game is one thing. But you don't know what's coming in the playoffs or how many games you might get to play. Somehow, throughout it all, Doug was still our best player, playing thirty minutes a game and making a difference every time he set foot on the ice. It made me determined to pull my weight. If a guy could go through something like that and still perform at a peak level, then I sure had no excuses.

The conference finals that year saw us facing off against the Vancouver Canucks, and we knew we were in for a fight. San Jose had taken us the distance in our conference semifinal series, and the physical play and cross-continent travel were taking their toll on our team. Now we had another West Coast team to contend with. Not only were the Canucks big, strong, and fast, but during those playoffs, goalie Kirk McLean played better than he ever had before. Vancouver had taken out the Dallas Stars in five games in their own conference semifinal, so they were more rested than us. Still, we came out swinging, and the first game dragged out to overtime. Peter Zezel scored late in the extra period to win us the game.

Walking back into the dressing room after our Game One win, I felt incredibly relieved, and we all seemed a little more confident. We knew that it would take all of our reserves to keep up with the Canucks, but we were willing to put it all out there, and we'd proven that not only could we go the distance in a game with the Canucks, but we could in fact beat them.

But the Canucks clearly felt the same confidence, and they held us off to win Game Two of the series. Then, on the Pacific Coast, we hit a new low. We didn't score a single goal in the third and fourth games. No matter what we tried, McLean stonewalled us, and we just couldn't tap into the offence that had supported us all season. When Game Five rolled around, our season was on the line. We knew it, too, and we threw everything we had at the Canucks. Our efforts were enough to push the game to overtime, but the extra frame didn't solve anything.

As we got ready to head out for a second overtime, every guy in the room had the same look in his eyes—we were determined not to roll over, and we knew that if we could just take this game, we'd have the home-ice advantage in the final two games of the series. We had a fantastic home record, so that would at least give us a fighting chance. But all our hard work and sacrifice just weren't enough. Only fourteen seconds into the second overtime period, Greg Adams knocked the puck past Felix Potvin to win the game and the series. As the fans at the Pacific Coliseum broke into cheers and the players celebrated in the corner, I watched Felix slump back into his net. That move said it all—we were broken, we were defeated, we were done.

Overtime is a double-edged sword. On the one hand, it's the most even playing field there is—everything that happened previously in the game no longer matters. If you were down before, you don't care how you got to the extra frame, you just care that you have a chance to win. But on the other hand, it can be the most abrupt, agonizing way to lose. A single bounce, a misstep, or a bad play can wipe out sixty or eighty minutes of solid team play. Winning championships is about how good your team is, but you can never forget that luck plays a part—fate, bounces, health, you name it. And we found out that no matter how badly you want to win, sometimes you just can't overcome the right combination of talent.

When I look back on those playoff runs, I have mixed memories. Fans remember what happened on the ice better than players can. They're seeing things take place in front of them, and they form memories as events happen. But we were playing in the moment, and when a game or series was over, we had to move on to the next one. There was always another shift, another game, or another season to focus on. I often couldn't remember the details of what I'd done until I saw highlights in the weeks, months, or years after the seasons had ended. For the fans, watching the game is their release, and it's pure fun. From the fans' perspective, as much as hockey is a sport, it's also entertainment. But when you're playing the game, when you're the one who's putting your body on the line, it's hard sometimes to see the game that way until you have the time and space to reflect back on it all.

I like to think we provided fans plenty of entertainment in 1993 and 1994. And we had a lot of success, even if we weren't able to bring home a Cup. Some people measure success by the number of championships that a player wins, and I'll always regret that I wasn't able to bring a Cup home to Toronto. But even though we didn't win a Cup, there was something very special about those teams. We fought the good fight, and there wasn't anything more we could have given—every bit of blood and sweat we gave was for the blue on the front of our jerseys. To me, that's the definition of success, and by that standard we were all winners.

7

Breaking Down

Checking in the NHL is an art. There is a proper technique that you have to follow if you want to do it right, and of course you are bound by the official rules. But if you want to be one of the best at checking, you sometimes have to step outside the box. And, most important, you have to be willing to suffer and sacrifice for it.

Some people say that hitting in hockey encourages violence, or that the speed of the game makes it dangerous. There may be truth to those claims, but as a player, a solid body check is just a tool. It allows you to hold up a forechecker, wear down an opponent, or create space on the ice. You don't want to use this tool all the time, but when you do pull it out, it has to work perfectly.

I never practised hitting; I learned to hit the way I did by playing the game, and I had been running guys over from my earliest years in hockey. The little coaching that I did receive about how to check well was a piece of advice to hit through the crest on the other guy's jersey. That was Hockey 101 when I played—when you went to hit a guy, you aimed for the centre of the chest. The theory was that a skater's hips and the centre of their chest move the least; their centre of gravity can't hide. Good skaters can feint with their shoulders or distract you with their hands and a tilt of their head, but their belly button isn't going anywhere.

You didn't just want to get a piece of the guy to knock him off the puck—you wanted to get all of him, knock him down, and send a message. By aiming for that dead-centre sweet spot, I could be sure of two things: no matter which way the other guy moved, I had him dead to rights, and the hit was going to hurt me as much as it would him, because we'd both be coming to a dead stop.

In a lot of ways, that realization—that giving a hit was as hard as taking one—was what kept us all from becoming too violent. It was kind of like mutually assured destruction; it made sure that everyone was held accountable for their own actions. That was the old-school way we policed ourselves.

That sort of checks-and-balances system came into play in April of my first season with the Leafs, when we faced off against Bruce Bell and the St. Louis Blues. We were in the St. Louis Arena, and a few minutes into the game, I stepped onto the ice on a line change that was happening on the fly. The puck was headed into the Blues' zone, and the winger I was replacing was coming to the bench, near the red line. I jumped out early, so I was way ahead of the play and the other skaters coming off the bench. Bell picked up the puck in his corner and started to curl behind the net. It looked like he was going to pull a Bobby Orr or Paul Coffey move, taking the puck behind his own net and skating all the way down the ice. But Bell had his head down, concentrating on settling the puck down on his backhand as he cruised behind his net, and it was that momentary lapse in awareness that gave me an opportunity. I don't imagine Bell saw me as I raced down the left wing towards him. I slipped behind his defensive partner, and then, just as Bell was about to come out from behind the net, I levelled him with one of the hardest checks I'd ever delivered.

It was a clean hit—my chest connected squarely with Bruce's chest—and Bruce was out cold immediately. Then all hell broke loose. I looked up and saw that Charlie Bourgeois was coming in to fight me. I didn't want to mix it up right there, though. I told Charlie, "We have to move. I'll fight you, Charlie, but let's get off your buddy's head here." I was standing right over top of Bell, and Charlie was trying to get at me, and I was telling anyone who would listen to give the medics room to tend to Bruce. I was ready to answer for my actions, but I didn't want to put a guy lying on the ground in more danger because of it.

In my first two years in the league, a good percentage of my fights were caused by me hitting a finesse guy on the other team. I would deliver my hit, understanding full well what the consequences would be. I knew I would have to answer to the other guys on his team whose job it was to defend the skilled players against guys like me. Some people might see those stakes, weigh the risk and reward, and then turn away, either out of fear, self-preservation, or the need to stick to a game plan. But I couldn't do that. I'd see the challenge, race towards it, and dive in, ready to take whatever came back at me in return.

Sometimes, what came back at me wasn't just one guy, though—it was five of them. In those situations, I relied on my teammates to have my back, and I would do the same in return. One night late in the 1980s, we were playing in Detroit when, as often happened, a shoving match devolved into a full-on line brawl. I was squared off with Bob Probert, while Bob McGill, Gary Nylund, Russ Courtnall, and Gary Leeman took on the other Detroit guys. As I was fighting Probert, I was keeping an eye on my teammates. I noticed that one of the Detroit players had Russ Courtnall in a choke hold, and it looked like Russ was having trouble breathing, so, as I was punching

Probert, I yelled across to the guy holding Russ, "If you don't him let him go, when I'm done here, I'm going to fucking kill you!" The guy must have believed me, because he let Russ go right away. I liked to settle scores. If there was anyone on the ice trying to bully my teammates, I was going to do something about it.

I learned all these lessons early on in my career. Early in my second season with the Leafs, we were playing Philadelphia in a close game, with the score tied 2–2 as we entered overtime. A few minutes into the extra frame, I saw Mark Howe in the Flyers' corner with the puck. I was circling out from behind the net, and as I curled up the boards, Howe turned towards me and I caught him dead on, running him over with a hit directly to his chest. Howe had been battling through some on-again, off-again injuries at the time, and an older player might not have followed through quite like I did. But I was young and didn't know any better, and it had been an emotional game, so I wanted to spark something and get our team going to carry us through the extra period.

Mark was probably the best defenceman in the league at that time after Paul Coffey, so I knew right away that somebody on the Flyers was coming for me. My hit had carried me forward and onto my knees, and the first thing I saw as I turned around was Ron Sutter coming down the wing towards me. In those days, after a hit like that, you owed the other team a fight, and I was willing to give it to them, so I figured Ron was coming to pay me back. I wanted to be ready, so I threw my gloves off and tried to grab him and get myself set for a fight. But Ron kept skating by. I was confused—I thought that, somehow, I was going to come away scot-free. But I couldn't have been more wrong.

The play was starting to move up ice, so I bent down to pick up one of my gloves. As I straightened up, I saw a blur of orange and black streaking towards me. Rick Tocchet had seen the hit, and he was sprinting from the other side of the ice towards me. I immediately dropped my equipment as he threw his stick and gloves to the side, and as soon as he was on me, we were throwing punches. Our momentum carried us right to the boards, where we stood, hammering away at each other for twenty seconds straight. We didn't strategize or try to do anything fancy. It was just a flurry of fists.

The Flyers knew that Mark had to be at his best for them to have a chance at a winning season. And for that to happen, they couldn't let anybody take liberties with him. So when Tocchet saw me hit the best player on his team, he knew he had to do something about it. Guys put a lot of stock in the codes, or unwritten rules, of hockey. Those do exist, and you have to respect them, but at the end of the day, you have to be able to stand up for yourself and the choices you make. You can't run from your problems in hockey. If I hadn't stood up for myself after I made that hit, someone from the Flyers would have jumped me anyway, or they would have targeted one of my teammates and used them as a scapegoat. And the refs would probably have let it happen. In that era, there was only one ref in charge of the game, supported by a couple of linesmen. We knew how each game would be called based on which referee was working that night. When I played, refs like Paul Stewart would allow just about anything. You could almost imagine a situation where three guys would be just about killed, and he'd just say, "Ah, let's call it a tripping penalty."

Good refs did a lot of talking. They would tell you flat out what to expect and what they were willing to allow. You knew exactly where you stood with them. They didn't want guys racing around, trying to hurt other players and then just walking away. That was bound to start a war that the guys in stripes would eventually have to clean up. If you tried that, a lot of old-school refs would quietly come over and say something along the lines of "Why are you running guys if you're not going to fight? I saw what you did—you started it!" They'd clear an area, let you and another guy settle things between the two of you, and then clean up the wreckage to get the game moving again.

As I skated off to the dressing room after my fight with Toc-chet, I realized that, if I wanted to make big hits like that one against Mark, I would have to stick up for what I did. For a long time, I was willing and ready to do that. I didn't want to stop playing physically. It was painful, and it was exhausting, but it helped my team and it gave me more options on the ice. So I kept throwing my weight around, trying to go bigger and better every game.

One of the biggest hits I ever gave out was to Chris Chelios in the 1994 playoffs against the Blackhawks. Chris was down in his end, coming up the right-wing boards. He had just passed the puck and was skating up the ice, watching his pass, when I came rushing down the wing. Just like Bruce Bell, Chelios never saw me coming, and I ran him over. Chelios was the main cog for Chicago at that time, so we wanted to make sure he was tired out at the end of every game. That was a common strategy. In a long series, instead of try-ing to keep the puck away from the best guy on the other team, we would actually try to get it to him. But although we would give him the puck, we wouldn't give him any time with it. By forcing him to handle the puck all game, every game, and putting pressure on him every time he was on the ice, he was bound to get worn down, tired, or scared, and eventually he'd make a mistake. Even the great-est players were human, after all.

While I gave out my fair share of hits in my career, I was also on the receiving end more than a few times. You try to forget most of them—imagine making a mistake like looking at your feet too long or admiring a pass you just made, and then having twenty thou-sand people cheer when another guy punishes you for that error. But some memories stuck with me, and I tried to use them as lessons. Every hockey player knows that you never carry the puck with your head down, but until you realize just how disastrous it can be to do that, there's a small part of you that thinks you can get away with it or that no one will catch you.

When I was in junior, Rocky Trottier nailed me right at centre ice as I carried the puck with my head down. You'd think I would remember never to do that again. But in my first year in the NHL, Larry Robinson stood me up at centre ice as I rushed up the middle. I only came up to Larry's chest, so when I ran into him at full speed, it was like hitting a brick wall. And then, a year later, Mark Messier did the same thing—again, right at centre ice. Needless to say, for a while there, centre ice was bad luck for me.

Each time I was hit hard like that, I didn't fall down. To broadcasters or fans at the time, it just looked like the other guy and I collided; it didn't seem that I had just been creamed. But the truth was, every time it happened, I could barely breathe. Anytime I took a big hit, I would skate to the bench, and it would feel like my guts had been liquefied and everything inside of me had come loose. It felt like my lungs were collapsed and wouldn't expand, no matter how hard I tried to suck in air. My ears would be ringing, and the ache would radiate across my body into every extremity. But I couldn't just sit there until I felt perfect again. A few minutes later, I'd be back out on the ice, ready to do it all over again.

There was only so long I could keep that up. Glen Sather had told me that, the way I was playing, I wouldn't last. Those words had stuck with me, but I had never thought about how I would actually go about proving him wrong. Then, one night after a game at the Gardens, I ran into Gordie Howe. I still had a reputation for fighting at the time, and Gordie knew it. He looked at me and said, "You're a good player. Don't accept that you *have* to fight all the time just because you think there's someone else coming. Fight when you *want* to fight. Fight on *your* terms."

When Sather spoke to me at the All-Star game, I was a young man and I hadn't spent much time considering the gravity of what he was saying. But when Gordie talked to me, I was more mature and I was ready to really hear it. Gordie's words made sense, and I knew that I had to change.

Nobody had ever made me hit or fight. In fact, I enjoyed it.

I loved the pure competition of a fight, just trying to outlast and overcome the guy across from me. The thrill was incredible. As a young player, I had felt like I could punch a brick wall as hard and as often as I wanted and it wouldn't hurt. At that age, I wasn't smart enough yet to know that it hurts! But as I got older, my mentality was changing. And given how hard the physical play was on me already, I decided I would pick my battles more carefully. If my hands and face were sore after a fight in Chicago against Behn Wilson one night, I would tell myself I wasn't going to run around the next night in Minnesota and fight Willi Plett there. I would change the way I played, just a little bit, because I couldn't answer the bell that night; my body wouldn't always take another fight. But even though I was becoming a smarter player, all the years of physical play and thinking myself unbreakable were still catching up to me.

● ● ●

There was no specific hit or fight that led to my first major back injury. For years, I'd been enduring aches and pains of one sort or another, and eventually, I played through so many injuries that my back finally said, "That's it." As I played through pulled groins, broken hands, and bad shoulders, I had to cheat—tweaking my mechanics—to compensate for those injuries. And every time I adjusted my technique, my body had to learn new muscle movements it wasn't used to. It became a snowball effect where every injury meant new techniques, which led to new injuries, and the result was that parts of me just wouldn't heal. My right hand was broken all the time—it got to the point that I started taping the knob of my stick until it was the size of a water glass, just so I wouldn't have to close my hand to pick it up. When my hands were that bad, I could hardly shoot. I would be on the ice with a massive roll of tape at the top of my stick so that I could skate without having to grip it.

But no matter what I was going through, I would never tell the coaches I was unwilling or unable to play. I knew that, as long as I got on the ice, I would find a way to contribute. I never wanted to miss a game or a practice, so I would do anything to adapt and recover enough to play. It was never for me to make the choice of whether or not I should be out there; I wasn't running the team. Each time I was hurt, I had a responsibility, as an athlete, to make the call myself and tell my coaching staff whether I could play or not. And like any true competitor, I'd say, "I have to go out." When asked if they can play or not, most players will say the same thing. Few would admit it, but just about any skater was afraid to come out of the lineup, because they had a fear of never getting back in.

In the NHL, you can play hurt, but you can't play injured. You're judged on how you play, and given the high level of competition in the league, if you're off by even the smallest degree, everyone picks up on it. The smart players are the ones who know when to push it and when to hold back, saving themselves for when it counts. I suppose I wasn't very smart. I played through a lot, and eventually my body went sideways.

When my body finally fell apart for the first time, I was out for a year. I missed one hundred straight games due to my back problems. I played a game in Philadelphia on February 4, 1988, and didn't play again until March 1, 1989. This wasn't just low-level discomfort that I could suffer through in order to play. I was in serious agony, and I had run out of ways of handling the pain by myself. I had to admit that something was seriously wrong. So, after the game in Philadelphia, I went in for a consultation with the team doctor. After running some tests and reviewing the results, the doctor told me the words that no one wants to hear: "You're not going to get better. My suggestion is that you seriously consider retiring." The X-rays revealed that there wasn't any structural problem with my back. It was more a case of overall body abuse that started when I played midget hockey and accumulated through junior and my time in the NHL.

At first, I was just angry that I'd have to miss a lot of playing time, although I never thought it would stretch as long as it did. I was also angry at my body for betraying me and for letting me down. I was angry at the doctor for suggesting that my time playing hockey could be done. It somehow felt like I had failed, and I was upset that I wasn't being offered any solutions. I was in my early twenties—my career had barely started, and I wasn't anywhere near ready to hang up my skates.

Even though it was the 1980s, our training staff's methods hadn't developed much beyond what was used in the 1930s. We had good doctors and surgeons, but we didn't really have the rehab specialists that we needed. For the most part, rehab was unheard-of when I first broke into the NHL. So I took it upon myself to start searching for answers. I went anywhere and everywhere in hopes of finding a treatment for my back that would allow me to play again. I got second opinions from the team doctors. When they confirmed the original diagnosis and advice, I decided to go outside the team for help. This was an unusual step in the 1980s. I was afraid the Leafs' doctors would tell me it was a waste of time trying to fix something that would never get better, so I didn't tell them what I was doing. It was my career and my body, and I knew I wasn't wasting my time. So, I got third opinions from physicians independent of the Leafs. When they proved to be no more help, I started seeing specialists. I went to see every osteopath everywhere from Toronto to Thunder Bay. You name them, and I went to see them. And when I had exhausted my options in Canada and still hadn't heard an answer I could accept, I went to professionals outside the country, like the ones at the Mayo Clinic in Minnesota. Weeks and months dragged on, and I still hadn't found someone who could help me. I never lost hope, though—to me, there was no extreme I wouldn't consider to keep playing hockey.

Then, finally, a breakthrough arrived. I was at home one day when Don Meehan called. Don had received a call from Ken Thomson, also known as the 2nd Lord Thomson of Fleet. Ken was a well-known Canadian media magnate and billionaire, and he was also a passionate hockey fan who loved the Leafs and had connections to the organization. When you have "Lord" as part of your name, you don't do things the way the rest of us do. He had reached out to Don after hearing about my back problems, and wanted to know if he could help.

I talked with Ken and explained how no one I'd seen had been able to provide a solution, so Ken invited me to travel to London, England, to consult with his personal osteopath, Dr. Lutchman "Billy" Naidoo.

I was blown away by Ken's generosity. He set up my travel, my accommodation, and all of my medical appointments. I arrived in London in late June 1988, when the Wimbledon tennis tournament was in full swing. For two weeks, I lived in London, where I spent my days as a sort of lab rat. I would go into Dr. Naidoo's office in the morning to run through a battery of tests. To my mind, Dr. Naidoo was one of the most advanced health-care professionals I had gone to see. And I trusted him and his team immediately. The specialists in London were quickly able to confirm that my body was completely out of whack from playing through so many injuries, and they confirmed the original diagnosis that my back would forever revert to a state of pain and injury because of the abuse it had taken.

I'd heard that from every other doctor so far, so it was nothing new, and just as it had every other time, hearing that diagnosis confirmed tested my confidence. But for the first time, I was also given reason to hope. Because, unlike every other doctor I'd seen until then, Dr. Naidoo had figured out a way to take my worn-down back and get it to a point where I could play again. Over the course of two weeks, Dr. Naidoo saw me every other day. By the end of my time with him, he was able to get me back in alignment. It wasn't a permanent fix, but I finally had a road that pointed back to the NHL.

It was made clear to me that it would be a long journey, though.

The two weeks in England were just the start of the process, and obviously I wouldn't be able to fly back and forth from London to Toronto on a regular basis for treatment. But I needed support. Dr. Naidoo told me that what I would need more than anything would be a soft-tissue specialist in Toronto, someone who would understand what I was going through and who could do the hands-on therapy that my injuries needed.

By the 1980s, professional hockey players were being paid more and more, but teams weren't investing in better training staff. The trainers were great guys, but not full-time professionals with years of schooling and training. On that score, things hadn't advanced much since the 1940s. There were great surgeons who could fix an injured knee, but once the player was out of the hospital, there was no rehab or support system to help them between then and the time they returned to the ice. So you would go from surgery to playing in no time at all. So, once again, I knew I'd have to look beyond the Leafs organization to find someone who could help me.

I found that someone when I met Chris Broadhurst, whom I mentioned earlier. I was thrilled when I discovered Chris working at a local sports rehab centre right at Yonge and College in Toronto. Chris was a trained sports medicine therapist, and he became a major reason why I was able to come back from my injuries at all. His talents meant that my career lasted twice as long as it otherwise would have. Luckily, the team also recognized what he was able to do, and at the end of the 1988–89 season, the Leafs hired Chris onto their staff.

Chris was the most advanced therapist I had come across to that date. He studied a wide range of ways to treat athletes, and he understood body mechanics, so he could tailor treatments to each individual athlete's needs. He definitely was the best therapist out there. I will be forever grateful for meeting him.

With everything finally in place, I was able to get back to playing hockey on a regular basis. It took Chris six months to get me ready to play, but it was all worth it. I didn't want to come back to coast on the ice or play small minutes. I was looking to make a difference. And to do that, I was going to have to pay a price very single day. Although the work that Dr. Naidoo and Chris were doing was incredible and allowed me to get back into the game, I had to face the fact that I would never again be 100 percent healthy. When I first came back from my injury, it took four hours of work a day to get my back in shape for the game. Even after my initial return, when my recovery wasn't as intense, I was still seeing Chris for at least an hour in the morning and then an hour at night; on bad days, it was twice as long. I would show up at 7 a.m. on game day for my first therapy session of the day.

The morning sessions were hard. My body was usually sorer and less flexible because it was early in the day and I hadn't warmed up yet, so that therapy was as important for my game-day preparation as taping my sticks or tying my skates. After a first round of daily therapy, I'd participate in the morning skate, go about my day, and then, at 4 p.m., I'd be back at the rink for a second session. Chris and I would adapt the afternoon treatment to however my body was feeling after the skate earlier in the day. Some of the time, everything would be clicking, and I could get away with some light rehab. Other days, it was as though my back was made of wood. My range of movement would be restricted, my legs would be aching from having to compensate for my back being out, and I'd generally feel as though parts of my body were locked into place and I didn't have the key that would let me regain control over them.

A lot of the time, to get over those problems, my second round of rehab involved acupuncture. I was heavily into direct acupuncture. I had needles stuck in me in all sorts of places, depending on the injury I was dealing with. It seemed an odd choice to a lot of my teammates at the time, but acupuncture had some of the best results for my back, and it was huge for me in terms of getting my body to work again.

There were setbacks, of course. During one acupuncture treatment session, the tip of a needle broke off in my leg. I only had myself to blame—I was experimenting with giving myself acupuncture, and I accidentally broke the needle. When I realized what I'd done, I tried to remove the needle tip, but I couldn't find it. The little metal shard stayed there for two years, lost and floating around in my leg. I would feel the prick from it at odd times, but it didn't really bother me too much. I only hoped that it wouldn't go into the bloodstream and start cruising around. Two years later, while I was playing for Quebec, I felt the needle poking out of my skin, so I went to the team doctor and told him what it was. I asked him, "Can I get this needle taken out?" He looked at me and said, "What are you talking about?"

As I explained to him what had happened, the doctor gave me a long, strange look, and his eyes widened as I pointed the spot on my leg and told him, "If you just cut right there, the needle will come out." So the doctor made a small incision in the skin, and there was this little acupuncture needle that had been missing for two years. He removed the inch-long piece of the metal that had broken off, looked at me, and asked, "That's been in you for two years?" as he shook his head in disbelief.

But through all the injuries, rehab, and physical play, I barely ever took painkillers. If Advil or Tylenol didn't do the trick, I would just endure the pain—I wasn't comfortable with taking anything stronger. There were all sorts of painkillers that were available to us at the time, but I didn't want to take anything that would affect my mood or my mind. I knew how to play well when I was hurting. I didn't know if I could do the same thing while on painkillers. And at the end of the day, I wanted to make sure I was sharp so that I'd be able to play.

Because, in my mind, that's what it all boiled down to—I loved playing hockey, and I would do anything it took to play. In life, you either like something or you love it. Playing hockey was something

I loved, and it was what I truly knew how to do. I had never had another job, and I didn't want one. There was never a Plan B for me, so I was willing to do whatever it took to make my hockey career last. Even as I lay on the table, pain firing through my legs as my back fought whatever new treatment it was going through, I had no regrets about the way I played. I loved the game and I only knew one way to play. I am the man I am today because of the way I played the game. And I wouldn't have been the only guy from my era who paid a physical price to play the game we love.

Looking back, if I had been smarter when I was a young player, I might have done some things differently. But I played the cards I was dealt, and the bottom line is that the pain, the lost time, and the rehab were all worth it.

8

Leaving Home

I n June 1994, I had just completed my ninth season in the NHL, all of them with the Toronto Maple Leafs. We had just come off our second deep run in the postseason, and I was the captain of the team. The previous season had even been my best year offensively—I'd scored forty-six goals. There had been rumours on and off from 1991 to 1993 that I might be traded. But in 1994, my stock was high, and after our recent playoff run, there was no buzz about me being dealt, so I had no reason to think the Leafs had any intention of trading me. Things couldn't have felt better, and I didn't expect anything to change anytime soon. But my life changed on June 28, 1994. That was the day when I was traded to the Quebec Nordiques for Mats Sundin as part of a blockbuster multiplayer deal.

For the first nine years of my career, playing in Toronto, hockey had been fun, plain and simple. Until you're traded for the first time, you never treat playing hockey as a job. It's only after you're traded that you truly understand the business side of the game. You may see friends and teammates come and go through trades, and you know that it's a part of the game. But it doesn't impact you directly, so you don't give it much attention. Once it happens to you, though, suddenly every other thing in hockey becomes part of the business. How you interact with your teammates, how you treat your body, how you perform in a season—to an extent, they all become points in a business deal.

June 28—the day I was traded to Quebec—was the date of the NHL Entry Draft, and I had been busy all morning shooting a Cheerios commercial. I'd been on the set all day, so I hadn't had chance to keep on top of the team's moves. On the drive home, I stopped at the Esso station at Front and Bathurst Streets in Toronto. As I filled my car up with gas, I turned on the radio and tuned in to a sports station to find out who we had drafted. But instead of hearing about the Leafs' draft picks, I discovered I had been dealt to the Nordiques.

I was floored. I sat in the car as the analysts went on about what the trade meant to the team. Part of what had me so shocked was that I hadn't even heard I was being traded. I didn't have a cell phone, and because I'd been away from home filming the commercial all day, nobody could get ahold of me when the deal was made. Cliff Fletcher had reached out to my agent, Don Meehan, hoping he might have a line to me. But Don had no way to get ahold of me, either, so there I was, the captain of the Leafs, hearing about my trade to Quebec for the first time over the radio at the Esso station.

I wasn't all that emotional at the time. As I sat in the car, I didn't have to put words to what I was feeling, so I didn't get choked up. In fact, I didn't know what to feel. Excited at a new opportunity? Upset that I was leaving the Leafs? Angry that no one had told me ahead of time? All I could think was, "Well, I guess I'm no longer a Leaf."

After hearing about the trade, the first thing I did was go to the beer store in the Molson brewery across the street and pick up something to bring home. When I got home, I had a million messages on my answering machine. That's when things started to sink in. As I had to return calls and talk to the press about the trade, it all came together and I started to get emotional. After I was up-to-date on all the details of the trade, I grabbed the phone. Todd Gill was the first guy on the team that I called. The next thing I knew, Giller and Dave Ellett picked me up and we all went out that night. Because it was the end of June, most of the guys on the team had left for their off-season homes. So for that night, it was just me, Giller, and Ellett, sitting around, drinking beer, and dealing with the news. But even as I sat there with my buddies, I could feel something had changed. I realized that, although I'd still have my friends from Toronto, I was now the property of another team.

The next day, the scene in Toronto got even crazier as the media started following me around everywhere. People were coming by the house so much that I couldn't find two seconds alone to think. Dave Ellett suggested that I get out of town for a bit and hide out. He drove me out to Grand Bend, Ontario, on Lake Huron, where we stayed with another teammate and friend, Dave McLlwain. But the escape was short-lived. Word got out that I was in Grand Bend, and all of a sudden the small town's main street was crowded with journalists looking for a photo or a sound bite.

The rest of the summer was a blur. I went through the usual logistical matters of finding a new home in Quebec City and getting everything packed up. I wondered how much French I'd need to be able to speak to play in Quebec. The first bit of the language that I learned was *chien chaud,* or "hot dog." The Nordiques' arena served the best hot dogs in the NHL, and now that I would be living there, I could have them seven days a week if I wanted to. I reminded myself not to go overboard—it would be hard to keep my weight down with easy access to such good junk food.

In August, not too long before I left for Quebec, the fans held a send-off rally for me at Mel Lastman Square in North York. I didn't know what to expect, but when I got there, I was overwhelmed by the turnout. The event was in the middle of the afternoon, in the height of the summer, and yet there were thousands of people in the square. I had wanted to do right by Toronto—the team and the city that had given me a life and a career—and lead the Leafs to a championship, and I was leaving without having accomplished that. So when I saw so many fans, all of whom had come out to show their support, I was touched. It was a magical moment I'll never forget.

A few days later, Dave Ellett helped me pack up my truck for my drive to Quebec. Dave was more than just a teammate, he was a good friend. That's when reality truly set in. I realized that I wasn't just leaving behind my teammates; I was leaving behind friends and familiar faces, and an entire life, too. It was a bittersweet drive along the highway to Quebec, to say the least.

● ● ●

Every hockey player will tell you that the first time you're traded, the game changes for you. When you join your first team, you're not just starting a new job, you're living a dream. There's nothing more important than what is happening to you right then and there, and you don't have the perspective to reflect on the bigger picture or the business aspect of the game. As I drove to Quebec, my perception began to change. To a certain extent, being a hockey player had become my job.

I should have been more prepared for the experience of being traded. Let's be honest: if you're playing in the NHL and you see Wayne Gretzky get traded, you should be prepared for anything. Because if the best player in the game isn't untouchable, then nobody is. But although I was caught off guard by the change of scenery, I knew that dwelling on the past was a sure way to hold myself back. Once a thing had happened, it was finished, and it was time to move on. I remained a team player, and I still wanted to win more than anything. And I began to think of my skills as a hockey player as something I could apply anywhere.

Reality sank in when I arrived at training camp and held my new jersey for the first time. I looked down, and instead of the Maple Leaf crest with a *C* by the left shoulder, I was staring at the Nordiques' fleur-de-lis. Although I was disappointed at having to leave Toronto, I was determined to make the most of my new situation. One great thing about being traded to a new team was that I was suddenly introduced to a whole new set of amazing people—office staff, training staff, players, and fans—all of whom would impact my life in some way. Playing with Quebec was my first introduction to the fact that, the more you move around the league, the more you meet all manner of people who make the game go around. And, for the most part, they are interesting and important.

When you enter a new dressing room, there's a period of adjustment as you figure out where you fit in the new group. It can take time to figure out what everyone's role is, who the leaders or jokers are, what makes each person tick. But when I joined the Nordiques, I learned for the first time that what you're really looking for is who the real hockey players on the team are. Everyone on a team is a hockey player, of course, but when hockey insiders—the pros, coaches, analysts, and everyone else who lives and breathes the game—describe an athlete as a *true* hockey player, they mean one thing: that guy can play. Some guys have practised and honed flashy skills. Some skaters have a specific role that they perform better than anyone else. But a real hockey player is a guy who has a feel for the game and knows it better than anyone who studied it ever could. They act on instinct—even when they can't tell you why they made a particular move, those players know they're right, because they can sense what to do. These are the players who are in the right spot all the time. They're the ones who may not impress you in a practice, but on game day, they show up and they deliver, which is all that should matter.

It took time for me to hone my sense of who those players were, but there was no shortage of candidates on the Nordiques in September 1994. The blockbuster trade in which the Nordiques had exchanged the rights to Eric Lindros for draft picks and prospects had just happened a couple of years before, in June 1992, and the talent Quebec had picked up was starting to develop. The squad I was joining was one of the best young teams you could find. Their real secret weapon was the rookie Peter Forsberg. Nobody in the league really knew yet just how good Forsberg was. Nobody except for the Nordiques' coaching staff, that is. When camp started, you could immediately see that Peter was something special. The first time I saw him handle the puck, I was amazed at how good he was. He had European training and skills, but he paired that with a North American attitude in that he liked physical play as much as he liked finesse. He was tough to handle.

While Forsberg was on his way to becoming a superstar, Joe Sakic was already there. Joe was a twenty-five-year-old western Canadian kid who had three one-hundred-point seasons in his first six years in the league. Beside him was Owen Nolan, a young power forward who could rack up both points and penalty minutes. And that was just the tip of the iceberg. You also had Adam Deadmarsh, Valeri Kamensky, and Mike Ricci. And from my generation, Paul MacDermid and Bobby Bassen were both there. I was only twenty-seven going on twenty-eight when I arrived, but Paul and I, along with Uwe Krupp, were already the old guard on the team.

Our coach was Marc Crawford. I knew him a little bit because of the time he and his top assistant, Joel Quenneville, had spent coaching in the Leafs' minor-league system, so it was a relief to see some familiar faces. Jacques Martin was the other assistant coach, and in those three guys you had three very different personalities. The difference between being an assistant coach and a head coach in the NHL is like night and day. The toughest thing is to go from being an assistant coach on a team to being its head coach. Once players have become comfortable with you as an assistant, they often have trouble seeing you as a head coach. And once you have been a head coach, as Martin had, it can be hard to take a job as an assistant and defer to someone else's vision and authority. Fortunately, we didn't have that problem in Quebec that year. It was clearly established that Crawford was the head coach and Quenneville and Martin were his assistants, and everyone knew their role on the team.

With all those talented players on the ice, I was excited to get out skating with them. It got even better when I had the chance to play alongside Sakic. Joe was proof that sometimes a person is just born with a gift. No matter how hard I worked, I could never have become a better player than Sakic. It wasn't a matter of willpower or wanting it more. But I discovered that Joe Sakic worked extremely hard at his game. He was one of the first guys to dedicate a lot of energy towards improving his fitness, but he did it modestly. To look at him, you wouldn't think that Joe was all that powerful. But he was incredibly strong, and he trained the whole year round. And he went about it all very quietly.

Along with his physical training, Joe was constantly practising his shot—he had as quick and accurate a snap shot as anybody, ever. Sakic understood how he needed to play the game, but he also considered everyone else's role. He was one of those guys who knew exactly what was going on with everyone on the team. He was a gentleman who carried himself with class on and off the ice, and he wanted to help guys however he could. Other players saw that and respected it. Joe had elite skill and a great work ethic, and he was a great teammate who had an intuitive feel for the game. That's what a

Hall of Famer is all about, and I could see it in Joe from the moment I joined the team.

• • •

With the level of talent I was playing amongst in Quebec, I began to wonder if my time there might be a turning point, the start of something big in my career. But suddenly, things came to a screeching halt.

In our final exhibition game of the 1994 preseason, I got hit. That wasn't anything new. I was shooting from a bad angle, and I was off balance as Ken Klee hit me, so I went headfirst into the boards. There was nothing dirty about it; it was just one of those things that can happen in a game. I might have been all right, but by sheer bad luck, as I went down, my helmet fell off, and as I fell towards the ice, my bare head hit the boards. I lay on the ice, and I could feel right away that something was very wrong. I was taken to the hospital, where I was diagnosed with a major concussion. It was one of the worst injuries of my career. I spent the night in the hospital, and then I didn't leave my apartment for two weeks. I stayed in a dark room the entire time until I finally felt able to venture out. When I walked across the street for the first time, I broke out into a full sweat. It was baby steps the whole way in my rehab.

Had it been a "normal" regular season, I would have missed a lot of time because of the injury. But the NHL locked out its players on October 1 that year, and we didn't start the season until January. The concussion was so bad that I would easily have missed forty games and might not have made it back before January anyway. Although the lost season was disappointing in a lot of ways, I was thankful for the extra time to rest, and the downtime helped me recover that much faster. I even felt good enough to head back to Saskatchewan to visit home for a little bit.

While I was out there, I found myself going hunting with Kelly

Chase, Don Meehan, and a couple of other buddies, just outside of Saskatoon. I'd never gone hunting before, so I was a bit out of my element. It was quite a sight—the hunting ground we visited was barely a mile from the airport, so there we were, shotguns going off as we watched the airplanes take off and land. We bagged a few geese and took them to a restaurant in Saskatoon called Seafood Sam's, where Sam himself cooked up the geese for us. When I returned to Quebec after that and the season finally did start up, I'd had enough recovery time that it looked to most people as though I'd never been hurt.

When the shortened season finally did start up on January 21, 1995, we won five straight games before our first loss, after which we went on another win streak that lasted seven games. Things were starting off exactly as we'd hoped, but there were more bumps along the way. The concussion wasn't the last of my injuries that year. I had other bumps and bruises that just added to the previous ones I'd suffered over the years. Before I had even got to Quebec, I had been forced to deal with injuries to both knees and a broken hand that I suffered during my time with the Leafs—and that was on top of my chronic back pain. Despite all that, I still managed to play thirty-seven of the forty-eight games that season. A little pain or discomfort hadn't stopped me yet.

I brought my love of acupuncture with me to Quebec, and I even managed to get one of my teammates, Craig Wolanin, into it. We got to the point where the two of us would even do self-acupuncture. I had spent so much time getting treatments over the years that I had trained myself how to perform acupuncture on my own body. At least, I *thought* I had trained myself and knew what I was doing; that broken needle showed me that I was nowhere near as qualified as the professionals. But it didn't stop me from continuing to try it myself, even though that's definitely not something you should try at home. I would sit in the trainer's room, shoving needles into myself in the areas of my body where I thought it would help. I would do it to demonstrate to Craig, and then he'd try it on himself. The rest of the guys thought we were whacked. They would take one look at Craig and me lying on the trainer's tables, jabbing needles into our legs and hips, and it would make them so queasy that they had to take off.

While we made the playoffs that year, the New York Rangers knocked us out in the first round in six games. It was a rough, physical series. In the first game, I tried to set the tone for the series when I delivered a hit on Sergei Zubov. The Rangers had the puck in their end and I was in on the forecheck. I had Zubov lined up perfectly, and just as he let his pass go, I nailed him in the centre of his crest with a classic open-ice hit. It got the team fired up in a hurry.

The Rangers came right back at us in Game Two, though. Partway through the game, things weren't going well for us. We were down, and the physical play was taking its toll on our team. At one point, Sergei Nemchinov and I were lined up opposite each other for a faceoff, and I decided that I needed to stir things up. I thought that, if I punched Sergei, it might spark him into a fight, and if I could rattle him, that would be one less threat to worry about in the series. Things didn't work out the way I'd planned, though. My punch to Nemchinov caught him off guard, and I nailed him near the back of the head. Instead of getting into a fight that would spark our team, I got thrown in the penalty box. The Rangers went on to win the game, 8–3, and on top of that, the league didn't look too kindly on my actions—it fined me five hundred dollars.

The Rangers won the next couple of games, so I continued to do whatever I could to keep us alive. When we were trailing three games to one in the series, I scored a goal and added an assist in Game Five as we beat the Rangers, 4–2. It was looking like we might be able to swing the momentum in our favour. But just two nights later, we lost Game Six in New York and our season was over.

Having a season cut short is hard. But this wasn't just the end of the Nordiques' playoff run; it was the end of the Nordiques themselves. That summer, the Quebec franchise transferred to Denver, Colorado, and was renamed the Avalanche. That was the start of a brand-new chapter for the team. Forsberg matured, Sakic continued to dominate, and Roy became unbeatable. In June 1996, just one year after our loss to New York, the Avalanche won the Stanley Cup.

Unfortunately, I wasn't there to see that happen. When I was first moved to the Nordiques, Don Meehan and I were confident that, if I came and played, the deal would be right. But when it came time to negotiate the contract, I guess there turned out to be a sticking point with what had become the Colorado front office. So, in October 1995—just four months after the franchise was moved—I was traded to the New York Islanders as part of a three-team trade with the New Jersey Devils that involved me, Steve Thomas, and Claude Lemieux.

The Islanders were coming off a losing season—the first of what would be a string of seven—when I arrived, so it was a different experience from playing in Colorado. Mike Milbury was the coach that year, and he was a tough one to play for. For the longest time, the team had only hired former Islander greats to be the coach. Mike, however, was an alumnus of the hated Boston Bruins. I don't know how well that went over with the Islanders alumni.

Even the team's jerseys were hard to deal with. This was the era when the Islanders wore those ugly "Captain High Liner" uniforms. The crest on those jerseys was so big that we used to have to break it in just to be able to wear the jersey. I would have liked to play for the Islanders when they had their original logo. But, as was the case when I'd arrived in Quebec, I refused to dwell on the difficulties of the new situation. I was willing to help out my new team in any way I could.

One of the most exciting parts about playing for the Islanders was that I was in the same division as Eric Lindros and the Philadelphia Flyers. When Eric came into the league, for about a six-year window I don't think there was a better player around. We played the Flyers three times in the first month of the 1995–96 season, and we were practically helpless to stop him. In those three games alone, Lindros had three goals and five assists.

But Eric was no different than anyone else in the league when it came to physical play. It will get you, no matter how big you are. When you play a physical game, and you're that talented, there are constantly guys coming to get you. And if you have the puck a lot, chances are you're going to have your head down at least once. Unfortunately, sometimes once is all it takes to leave lasting damage. Eric took some big hits from a lot of nasty players around the league. All those hits add up and take a toll on a player, even someone as strong as Eric.

It's amazing how big a role personality plays on the ice. Sometimes, if a guy is a gentleman on the ice, players will just try to knock him off the puck instead of lay him out. Wayne Gretzky used to talk to you all the time on the ice. He would chitchat with everybody, all of it friendly. Wayne knew that if the guys on the other team liked him just a little bit, they'd hit him, but they wouldn't kill him. Anytime you're on the ice, there are twenty guys on the other team watching what you do to their teammates. You wanted to play with intensity, but you had to remember that if you crossed a line, someone was going to come for you, whether that was in the next game, the next month, or even the next season.

● ● ●

I wasn't in New York for long. On March 13, 1996—after scoring twenty-four goals in fifty-eight games with the Islanders—I was traded back to the Leafs as part of a multiplayer deal. I was thrilled. I couldn't wait to get back into the Blue and White. My first game back with the team was two days later, on March 15, when we hosted the Dallas Stars at Maple Leaf Gardens.

That was a special night in my career. Just to be back wearing the Maple Leafs uniform felt right. And to be back in the Gardens was even better. But underneath my excitement was uncertainty. I didn't know what to expect from the crowd. I wasn't sure if the city would be eager to see me again, or if I'd been gone for too long. I wanted to show my teammates that I was ready to earn back my spot on the team, that I didn't think my past with the team entitled me to special treatment. I wanted to prove my worth all over again to the people who were there now.

As I stepped out onto the ice for the warm-up skate, I remember that the building was really jumping, and I felt myself settling into a familiar zone more easily than I'd expected. Everything came together nicely that night after that. Early in the game, Doug Gilmour fed me a beautiful pass in front of the net and I wristed the puck upstairs for the first goal of the game. It was as though I'd never been gone. We didn't look back from there, and we went on to shut out the Stars, 3–0. I was even named the game's first star. I skated onto the ice after my name was announced, and as I heard the crowd's cheers, I started pumping my fist. I've never been one for showboating, but I couldn't hold it in—I was home.

● ● ●

My second stint in Toronto featured a mix of the old and the new. I picked up right where I left off with the friends I'd had to leave a couple of years earlier, including Dave Ellett. But coming back to Toronto gave me a chance to spend a lot of time playing with Kirk Muller. Kirk is one of those guys who don't just like playing hockey—they love it. Kirk would do anything to keep playing. He was drafted immediately after Mario Lemieux, making him the second-overall pick of the 1984 draft, and he put up big points for his first five years in New Jersey. Towards the end of his career, he became more of a role player, adapting to whatever spot the team needed him in, whether that was on the fourth line or the first. He was even a healthy scratch some nights. He was doing anything he could just to keep playing, because he loved it that much. Not many stars of Muller's calibre could put their ego aside and accept being a healthy scratch on a regular basis. But Kirk could, and I had enormous respect for him because of that.

In an interesting twist, one of the best parts of coming back to Toronto was also the reason that I was sent away in the first place: Mats Sundin. Mats was a typical Swedish guy—he left everything on the ice. Guys like Sundin and Forsberg struck me as very Canadian in the sense that they let their play speak for itself. Mats was our best player every night, and it didn't matter if you were one of the most skilled skaters, one of the training staff, or anyone else, he treated you with the same courtesy and respect. Mats was one of the most low-key superstars you'll ever see, and when your best player behaves that way, every other guy in the dressing room tries to live up to his example.

I had a lot of respect for Mats. When he was named captain of the Leafs, he took a lot of criticism from the press for not being exactly like the guys who had come before him—like Dougie Gilmour or Darryl Sittler. That was totally wrong, but to Mats's credit, he never rebutted or argued. And in the end, his stats and accomplishments proved to everyone just how good he really was.

In my first year after returning to the Leafs, we made it to the playoffs but lost in the first round to the St. Louis Blues. They ended up beating us in six games. From a distance, it looked like it was a close series, but when I was in the thick of it, it didn't feel that way. The Blues had Wayne Gretzky, Brett Hull, and a number of other talented players. Because of our deep playoff runs in 1993 and 1994, the bar had been raised a lot higher in Toronto. That's what you want as a team, and that's what we were aiming for, so losing out in the first round wasn't good enough for us. But while I hated losing, I was happy to be back home and playing for the Leafs. I could see the right sorts of things coming together on the team, and I looked forward to another opportunity to compete with them the next year.

It was around this point in my career that I started to experiment with the curve on my stick. I found that the better my back felt, the less curve I needed on my stick. When I was healthy, I could wrist the puck like I always had, and there was nothing to hold back my release. The worse my back felt, though, the more I resorted to snapping the puck and taking slap shots. I actually had two sets of sticks ready to go for every game—the "good back" sticks and the "bad back" ones. On the days my back felt bad, I would fire up the torch before the game and increase the curve of the blade on my sticks so that I could still shoot the puck the way I wanted to. It became just another piece of fine-tuning that I had to add to my therapy, rehab, and warm-up regimes to prepare for each game.

I must have had the curve on my stick just right on November 9, 1996, the night that I scored four goals in a 7–3 win over the Oilers. Curtis Joseph was in net for the Oilers that night, and it seemed that every puck I shot was going in. I realized it was my night when I scored one of my goals from the left-side hash marks. I was following my usual technique—aim for an area of the net, release as fast as possible—and all I was trying to do was hit the net. But the puck found its way to the far corner and went bar down for a goal. When you see that happen, you just know that the hockey gods are in your favour that night, and so you run with it.

The very next night, I had a ringside seat for the best goalie fight I ever witnessed. We were in Philadelphia to face the Flyers. It was a heated game and there were plenty of scraps—I had seventeen penalty minutes. But that wasn't the real news from that game. All that anyone could talk about after the game was the fight between Felix Potvin and Ron Hextall. I was on the ice at the time, and I knew something was going to happen. I was fighting Daniel Lacroix when I saw Hextall hurtle down the ice towards Felix in the corner.

I remembered the Hextall temper I'd seen in junior, and I could see it all about to unfold. I thought to myself, "Oh God, we have to get over there to help Felix." But only a few seconds into the fight, we all stood back—it was clear that Felix didn't need our help. None of us had any idea that Felix could fight. He was such a mild-mannered guy, and he never talked all that much. Later on, we found out that his dad had done some fighting in Quebec, the old bare-knuckle stuff. It turns out Felix knew how to take care of himself better than any of us ever imagined.

Don Cherry had a field day that night—it was his kind of game. I respected Don, and I especially liked the fact that he was such a pro-Canadian guy. I liked Don's honesty—I didn't have to agree with absolutely everything he said, but I knew he believed in what he was saying and that it came from the heart. And no matter what Don said, you wanted to hear what was going to come out of his mouth— it's what makes him such a great entertainer.

Over my playing career, I was lucky enough to interact with Don many times. In the old Gardens, Don and Ron MacLean's studio was right across the hallway from our dressing room. So, if I was hurt during the first period, I would just walk across the hallway and watch the game with Don and Ron in the studio. We would be sitting there, watching the game, and Don would lean over and say, "Watch what I say tonight!" He loved to tip me off that he was going to have something good to say on "Coach's Corner" that night.

It was the little moments like that that I'd missed when I was away from Toronto, the times when being at the rink or getting ready for a game didn't feel like just arriving at the office to do a job. It was refreshing coming back to a new team, too. When I returned, the whole team was in a transition. Pat Burns was gone, Doug Gilmour had been traded to New Jersey, and Mats had taken over from Dougie as the captain. The whole team was being overhauled.

Because of that, I knew that my role would be different. I wasn't the captain anymore, and I was perfectly fine with that. We had incredible leadership around us, and I recognized that my place in the dressing room and on the ice would be different from when I'd left. The change felt good, though, and it felt right being back in the Gardens, with both new and familiar faces around me. It was where I wanted to be. But what I wanted and what had to happen would prove to be very different things, and before long, the business of hockey would see me moving once again.

9

Journeyman Years

As much as I loved being back in Toronto, it was clear that my second stint with the Leafs wasn't going to last forever. My injuries were keeping me out of the lineup more and more often—I got into just forty-seven games in 1997–98—and we'd had a couple of disappointing seasons, missing the playoffs in 1997 and '98. I got the sense that, whatever rebuilding plans the team might have, I wasn't going to fit into them.

I was torn. On the one hand, I loved the team and the city. But I also felt that I had a lot of fight left in me, and I knew that I needed to find a team where I could play a meaningful role. So, when my contract with the Leafs was up, I made the difficult decision to shop my skills around.

On July 31, 1998, I signed as a free agent with the Tampa Bay Lightning. When I arrived in Tampa, the Lightning had only been in the NHL for six seasons. When they first joined the league, the

Lightning played their home games at Expo Hall, which only seated about ten thousand. In year two, they moved to what is now Tropicana Field, a domed baseball stadium. I was glad that they at least had a real arena by the time I got there.

The 1998–99 season turned out to be one of the more productive seasons of my career. I scored twenty-eight goals with the Lightning, enough to lead the team, and then four more with the Red Wings when I was acquired by Detroit in a trade-deadline deal. Even better, I was healthy enough to dress for seventy-seven regular-season games, the second-highest number of games played in a season in my career.

Those successes didn't just happen—I had to earn them. Dressing for that many games was a grind, but I had one major advantage: I was playing in Tampa, Florida. My body felt great playing in the warm weather. It's no mystery why so many people move down to Florida after they retire: they feel good in the morning. They wake up, the weather is nice, and their minds and bodies feel better because of it. When I was playing in Tampa, I wasn't nearly old enough to retire, but my body was showing plenty of signs of wear and tear, so the weather had the same effect on me.

The never-ending battle to maintain my back and my body in game condition continued. But when I woke up in the mornings in Tampa, my back wasn't in the same agony that it usually had been when I played in other cities. And because my body was doing better, my mind was in a better place. It was hard to stay upset during a tough stretch of games when I woke up and there were blue skies and perfect weather around me. And as I would drive to the rink with the window down and my elbow out the window, it would put me in a better position mentally to handle a stressful situation at the rink—whereas in the same situation in Canada, when it might be the fourth day of a snowstorm and you haven't seen the sun in three weeks, it becomes a lot harder to put yourself in a positive mindset. Given how much pain my back was still causing me day in and day out, I was thankful for the benefits the new environment gave me—I needed every bit of help I could get.

While the weather was helpful, so, too, was playing for Jacques Demers, the coach in Tampa at the time. Jacques was very much a players' coach. He cared more about connecting with and motivating his players than he did about rigidly sticking to a system. One of the most important things Jacques did for me—particularly at that stage in my career—was also the simplest: he let me take days off. He would look at me and ask, "Do you need today off?" Of course I wanted to be on the ice, competing and training with my team. But on the days when my body held me back, there was never a problem with Jacques. He would simply say, "Go rest, just as long as you're good to go tomorrow."

Jacques had coached veterans in St. Louis and Detroit, so he understood older players, and he knew that a mental break from the game is as much of a help as a physical one. Some of the newer coaches felt that being a leader required making an immediate impact. They wanted to leave their mark or set the tone right away, and that trumped what the players themselves needed. As a captain, I had learned that you have to listen to the people around you if you're going to understand their needs. You can't just take one solution and apply it to every person, team, or situation. The needs of the team come ahead of everything else, and managing that wide range of priorities takes patience and compromise. Jacques understood that, and I was thankful for that. The way that Jacques handled my situation showed just what an intelligent and experienced coach he was. Jacques knew players and his ability to handle players and people was admirable— anyone who lasts that many years in the NHL has some seriously impressive qualities. You don't just keep tricking people year after year.

A veteran coach like Jacques knew that understanding players was as important as understanding the mechanics of the game, and that season, I needed the type of communication and flexibility he provided. For instance, I never wanted to practise immediately after getting off of a flight. We travelled a lot, and a lot of coaches would schedule a practice right after the flight to get the team loosened up. But working out hard after flying was just too much of a physical strain for my body to take, and I ended up feeling worse because of it. In those later days of my career, less was more. Overpractising was a big no-no, because my body could never recover. I also knew I needed time between games to get ready, and Jacques worked with me to get me the time I needed. If we had games on back-to-back nights or a coach who decided that the solution to a loss was to plan more demanding practices, I was in trouble.

Practices in particular had become difficult for me—they bothered me physically as much, if not more, than games. In a game, I was only playing for fifteen minutes. But when we practised for an hour and a half, I was wearing myself down every minute. The same went for morning skates on game days. Afternoon games were perfect for me, because they meant we didn't have a morning skate—I could just go out and play my game. A lot of players didn't like afternoon games because they interfered with their routines. They were used to playing at night, and they often found it hard to wake up and get going on a different timetable.

Some people call them superstitions, but a superstition and a routine are two different things. Superstitions distract you. They add to your anxiety and take your attention away from the important things. Routines are calming. They allow your body to accomplish what it needs to, even when things aren't feeling right because you're sore, you're tired, or whatever, and you can still perform. Your mind and your body are accustomed to the repetition; there are times when it is the routine that gets you through. My routines—the way I taped my sticks, the rehab I did each morning—were my comfort zone. I'd repeated them so much that they didn't take any thought. I could just sink into familiar patterns and let them get me to the game.

It was a challenge to balance my need to recover and take things slow with my craving for competition. Every day was a battle, but every day, I would also wake up and remind myself that I was going to play hockey that day, and that made it all worth it. My love of the game never faded. So while practices were painful or travel was draining, I still looked forward to it all. Although it became difficult for me physically, travelling to away games was one of my favourite parts of any season.

Chicago was my favourite road city. I loved getting into town, staying in the Drake Hotel, and eating with the team at Gibson's Bar & Steakhouse. When I was playing with Tampa, though, I noticed that road trips had changed. Instead of going out to sit down for dinner together, guys on the team would head out in small groups and bring food back to their rooms, or they'd go to the movies. I would say to the young guys on the team, "You worked that hard to make it to the NHL just to go see a movie?" I figured I had my entire life after I retired to go and see movies. While I was still in the Show, I wanted to be totally immersed in that world, enjoying time with my teammates and experiencing as much as I could. I knew by that point that my time as a pro athlete wouldn't last forever, so I wanted to enjoy and make the most of every second of it.

On top of the weather being restorative and Jacques Demers being great to play for, there was another memorable aspect to my season in Tampa: Vincent Lecavalier was my centreman. Vinnie was an eighteen-year-old rookie that year, and he hadn't even filled out yet. As a rookie, he was six foot three and weighed maybe 185 pounds. When he won the Cup in 2004, he had bulked up to 225. That extra forty pounds meant you couldn't get him off the puck. When I joined the Lightning, the owner at the time, Art Williams, said that Lecavalier would be the Michael Jordan of hockey. We all just put our hands over our faces when we heard that. Talk about putting pressure on a kid.

With a skilled player like Lecavalier around, the rest of us had a responsibility to protect him and make sure he had the time and space to make a difference on the ice. That meant that any time the opposition looked to get in Lecavalier's way, we had to clear a path by playing tough, laying down hits, and fighting where and when it was needed. But where in previous years I would have been at the front of every one of those charges, I only fought once in 1998–99. I knew that, if I was the one fighting every night, it wouldn't be long before I was done for good. So I held back, trying to find ways to use my body efficiently and effectively. The wisdom that comes with age was finally starting to arrive.

● ● ●

The Lightning didn't draw great crowds that year, and their first sell-out crowd was on March 19, when the Red Wings were in town. We were excited that the place was packed, and in the dressing room beforehand, everyone was feeling good. We couldn't wait to get out in front of a huge home crowd. When we stepped out onto the ice that night, there must have been nineteen thousand people there . . . and they were all wearing Detroit's red jerseys. It was spring break, and everyone at the game was an out-of-towner in Tampa for the holiday. So much for the home-ice advantage. We lost 5–3 that night, but we had to laugh about it in the dressing room after, and my personal silver lining was that I'd scored a hat trick.

A few nights later, on March 22, I picked up an assist as we beat Wayne Gretzky and the New York Rangers, 6–3. For a team that was in last place overall, we seemed to be picking up steam and having fun, and I was feeling so good that I was scoring goals at a regular pace. I thought that things were looking up and that I'd end the season in Tampa. But the Lightning management had other ideas, and the morning after our win over the Rangers, I was traded to the Red Wings.

At that time, the three dominant teams in the Western Conference were Detroit, Colorado, and Dallas. Each was a regular Cup contender, and they played against each other often in the playoffs, which meant the rivalry amongst them was intense. The year before I was traded to Detroit, they had won their second straight Stanley Cup, and they were looking to make another deep run in the playoffs. That Detroit team in the late 1990s was a dynasty, full of future Hall of Famers like Chris Chelios, Steve Yzerman, Brendan Shanahan, Sergei Fedorov, and Nicklas Lidstrom.

Lidstrom, a defenceman, was one of the smartest players I knew. Everything he did on the ice seemed very unassuming, but he executed it so perfectly. He played in the NHL for twenty years, but when he retired, he was in better shape than probably 90 percent of the guys still playing, all because he knew how to make a difference using his brains, rather than relying on his brawn. Chelios, who joined the Wings the same day I did, also had incredible endurance— that guy's body has to be donated to science. Chelios broke into the NHL in 1983–84, and he only stopped playing in April 2010, when he was forty-eight. And it's not like Chelios stayed out of the traffic. He worked and played hard, but he was also one of those guys who were just a ton of fun to be around. Still, no matter how much fun he might have, you could count on him to be ready to get down to work the next day.

Over the course of my career, there were plenty of guys who could party late and still play hard at the rink the next day. They would just get on the bike before a game and burn the previous night out of their system. You would never know what they had been up to just a few hours earlier. But that sort of lifestyle wasn't usually sustainable. There were some guys I played with whose careers could have lasted five years longer if they had taken the game more seriously. They may not admit that to themselves, but it's true. Other guys are just the opposite—they find a way to keep going no matter what challenges they face. Gary Roberts is the perfect example of that. He was in his late twenties when he suffered a serious neck injury and had to go through intense rehab. And when he'd finally recovered from the injury itself, he had to completely overhaul his training regimen and diet to get his performance level back to that of an elite professional athlete. But because of all his hard work, he was able to play until his early forties with a body that probably felt like it was only in its twenties. That is the definition of dedication.

I had found out early in my career how far I could go and still be effective. I respected my job and the people I did it with. To me, being a hockey player meant being the best on the ice that I could. That's what I signed up for. Of course, there are going to be nights when you're not at your best—nobody is going to have eighty-two good games. But you have to *try* to have eighty-two good games. The attempt to be good every night has to be there; the game comes first, and you only get results through hard work. So if I wasn't going to put myself in the best situation to succeed, then I wasn't doing justice to my job, my team, or my sport. There's no doubt that Chelios did the sport and his team justice every time he stepped on the ice. He was a true professional.

The most impressive thing about that Red Wings team was that we didn't just rely on a few star players—there was a lot of depth. Kirk Maltby, Kris Draper, Darren McCarty, and Joey Kocur are just a few of the guys who played important roles. Everyone on the team knew what their job was, and when everyone did their piece, the team was unstoppable. Guys like Maltby, Draper, and Kocur also ran the dressing room. They had big personalities and were perfect for it. Lots of those guys could have gone to other teams and had a chance to be bigger stars. But they wouldn't have won all those Cups. The drive to win kept us all together.

And then, of course, there was the guy who made the Red Wings a true powerhouse: the captain, Steve Yzerman. The answer to why Stevie Y was such a legendary player—and why he's so good as a general manager now—is simple: he put in the hours. I'd never seen anyone work as hard to succeed as Stevie, and it showed. He lived and breathed the game. Steve was not only a great hockey player, he was very much a student of the game.

And leading them all was the incredible Scotty Bowman. As great a captain as Yzerman was, Scott was the undisputed boss in Detroit. Being the guy that he is, Scotty didn't say anything to me when I arrived in Detroit. I was there to play, and that's about it—we didn't need to be friends. I was fine with that, because his style worked for me. Scotty knew how to tailor his practices to suit the needs of his players. Some of the shortest and easiest practices I ever had were with Scotty Bowman in Detroit. For a team that didn't practise very hard, the Red Wings were all in great shape, which I saw as a testament to their individual dedication to being the best they could be. I had tried to channel that same diligence over the years, so I felt like I was in good company.

My first game with the Red Wings was on March 24, and I scored as we beat the Sabres, 2–1, at the Joe Louis Arena. Over the last twelve games of that regular season, we went on a 9–2–1 run, which gave us some serious momentum heading into the playoffs. I was loving the high level of competition.

With Detroit in the Western Conference, I was getting to play against teams and athletes that I used to face a lot with Toronto—in particular, Brett Hull. I had played against Brett a lot when he was in St. Louis and I was with the Leafs, and I knew that he was incredibly skilled in every part of his game. People used to think of Brett as a one-dimensional player, a pure goal scorer, but when he wanted to apply himself, he was an unbelievable athlete who could pass the puck as well as he could shoot it. That athleticism made him a threat every time he was on the ice. He would shoot the puck from anywhere—bad angles, direct angles, outside the red line, up close—and he always seemed to know instinctively where the net was.

Brett would practise spinning and shooting the puck as hard as he could. He wasn't trying to pick corners or do anything fancy. He just wanted to get the puck to the net as hard as he could. By practising that move repeatedly, he could do the same thing in a game and be on target every time. And given how hard Brett Hull could shoot the puck, that's all he had to do: hit the net. And the more I played, the more I came to realize that the old mantra of "Get the puck on net" was true no matter what level you played at.

Well, we were hitting the net, and we were scoring, and before we knew it, the playoffs were on us. We beat Anaheim in four straight games in the opening round, and then we faced off against Colorado in the second round. We took the first two games of the series, and as we headed back to Detroit, we didn't feel like anything could stop our momentum. You'd think that all that success would mean the Detroit media was really excited. But during that entire playoff run, there were never more than three reporters around after our practices. When the Leafs had a playoff practice, there would be dozens of reporters on hand. And that isn't even counting all the fans outside the rink. The Red Wings that year were a team of historical importance, and only three reporters were interested in talking with them. I was surprised, but I didn't see it as a bad thing, because it meant we could focus on what mattered: winning hockey games.

It looked like we were on track to do just that as we headed into Game Three against Colorado. But then things started to fall apart. Two things derailed our postseason that year: our goalie, Chris Osgood, got hurt, and at the same time, Colorado netminder Patrick Roy woke up.

There were three goalies I played against who stand out above the rest. Early in my career, Grant Fuhr was the guy to beat, and just before I retired, Martin Brodeur reigned supreme. But in the years between them, it was Patrick Roy all the way. Lots of goalies can step up their game to a higher level when the series is on the line. But when Patrick Roy got into one of his zones, he was practically unbeatable. And that's exactly what happened in the 1999 playoffs. Patrick Roy shut the door on us.

All of a sudden, it was awfully tough for us to score goals. The rest of the Avalanche recognized Roy's incredible play, and they rallied around him to protect him. I remember battling a lot with Avs

defenceman Adam Foote in front of their net. I had been a teammate of Adam's when he was a rookie in Quebec. We had even been
roommates on the road. He was a big man, and a fierce competitor—
and the fact that we were former teammates didn't matter to Adam.
He wasn't about to cut me any slack, and he made life miserable for
me anytime I went anywhere near Patrick Roy. Over the last three
games of the series, Roy gave up only four goals. That's why he's in
the Hall of Fame. We were outscored 14–4 in that span, and the Avs
won four straight games to take the series.

Once again, my playoff experience had been cut short. Another
year was over, and I was still searching for a chance to play for the
Cup. The coaching I'd received and my teammates in Detroit had
felt like a good fit, and I was ready and willing to make another run
with them the next season. I looked forward to the summer, was
ready to nurse my injuries and recover for another campaign. I was
ready to keep fighting, and I was far from done. Or so I thought.

10

Making an Exit

After going deep into the playoffs with the Red Wings, I was hoping that I would start the next season with the same team so that we could build towards another Cup run. I was a free agent, though, so there was no guarantee I would have a spot on the roster. I thought that I had a strong case to be re-signed, given that I'd just scored thirty-two goals the year with Tampa and Detroit and been durable enough to play seventy-seven games. But the Red Wings felt otherwise, deciding that they didn't want to risk signing me.

The sting of being rejected by a team never goes away, even as an older player. You can't help but take it personally. I could have given in to self-pity, but that would have done nothing to help me. By that point, I was able to see things more clearly from the perspective of management. If I'd been in my prime as a player, tied up in my own career, I might have been upset with other people not seeing things exactly as I did. Time and experience help to change your point of view, and as an older player, I could understand the general manager's thought process. Do they dress a twenty-two-year-old who has upside and can continue to develop into a greater talent? Or, for the same money, do they dress a thirty-two-year-old who has experience, but serious health risks as well? It was a risk-and-reward calculation.

Still, after the Red Wings passed on signing me, I had confidence that I would find the right team to play with for the 1999–2000 season. But as the summer wore on and I hadn't been signed with a team, things became more and more uncertain and I got increasingly nervous. I wasn't ready to retire yet, and I was willing to play just about anywhere, in any role, if it meant I got to keep lacing up my skates.

It wasn't until August that I was given the opportunity to continue playing hockey. The most powerful guy in the NHL, the late Bill Wirtz—also known as "Old Man Wirtz"—and the Chicago Blackhawks agreed to sign me to a one-year deal. I was thrilled, and I couldn't wait to get to training camp. The coach in Chicago that year, Lorne Molleken, was young and new to the NHL, so he was strict. His practices were harder than any game we played. There were other veterans on the team that year, including Doug Gilmour, and we knew we were going to be pushed to keep up.

Mentally, I was ready for the challenge, and I looked forward to seeing what new depths I could tap. But my body had other ideas. Only a couple of days into camp, I hurt my groin while skating. I knew that I had a lot of work ahead, though, and that the Blackhawks were taking a chance on me, so I kept my injury quiet. I didn't tell anyone and just played through the pain. Of course, that meant I wasn't playing as well as I could have, so I didn't make the impression I wanted to.

I was in my thirties by now, and rehab was taking up more and more of my time. As an athlete, your body is supposed to serve you.

When it rebels, like mine was doing, each outburst takes longer and longer to put down and get over. This time around, it took me two months of skating on my own before my groin healed and I felt good enough to play. At that point, though, we were well into the season, the roster was set, and there wasn't a spot for me on it. And so, just before Christmas, when the Blackhawks put me on waivers and nobody claimed me, they released me from my contract. Just as I had been a few months earlier, I was back to floating in uncertainty.

There are many stages in your career as a player when you really need your agent. As you get to the end of the line, a good agent is invaluable. Fortunately, I had the best in Don Meehan. In my opinion, you and the person who represents you have to hit it off. You don't want a personality conflict, because ideally, that agent is going to be working for and with you forever.

There's a stereotypical idea that agents are always about the dollar. And there are times when you need that sort of killer instinct working on your behalf. But a great agent also knows when to place the bigger picture above a paycheque. There's more to a career than just getting the most money at a particular moment. You have to think about where you'll play the best, because when you play your best, it means that people notice your efforts and give you opportunities to play longer. Success breeds success.

I always received an honest answer from Don; he simply wouldn't blow smoke, and he never talked about a deal just to pocket another fee. If a player told Don what he wanted to earn and Don didn't think it would be possible to get it, he'd be straight up and say, "We can ask for that. But you're not going to get it." Don would tell you what you needed to hear, not just what you wanted to hear. Not every contract is going to be a blockbuster deal. Don also recognized that every player was an individual, and there was no cookie-cutter solution that would apply in all cases. Don wanted the best for his guys, and he would do whatever he could to make sure they were in the right environment at the right time to succeed. I respected Don's savvy and his loyalty. For me, just as with Don, somebody's word is more valuable than a dollar. Money comes and goes. But a reputation lasts a long time.

When the Blackhawks released me from my contract, I was starting to think that my time in the NHL was up. But I wanted to keep playing, and Don knew that. He also knew which teams were looking for help, and so he started making calls and working the contacts he'd amassed over thirty years, trying to find me a place to play. You can't buy that kind of dedication.

Meanwhile, I had rented a place in Chicago for the full year, so I stayed there to train and get healthy. I kept my training routine simple, focusing on overall fitness and some weights here and there. I usually didn't lift weights during the winter because they hurt my hands. I had noticed that when I lifted weights during the season, my hands felt stiff and wooden when I tried to handle the puck. From what I had seen, the Europeans had figured out an ideal way to train for hockey well before we did in North America. I watched a lot of Canadians and Americans doing "beach body" workouts— they made you look good from the waist up, but from the waist down, the usual choices were running or biking, which were fine, except that they weren't the best way to become a better hockey player. It made sense to me to do more weight lifting that focused on the legs. After all, that's what I was relying on when I was on the ice. No matter what my exact workout was, though, I liked to work out alone so that I could concentrate on what I was doing without distractions like chitchatting neighbours or horsing around with friends.

On top of my gym work, I rented ice so that I could skate by myself, and I continued with the hours of rehab that had become such an important part of my life. Those were long, difficult days. I hated watching the NHL season being played out from the outside. I felt like I was in limbo. I needed a way to channel my energy, so every time I went to the rink or the gym, I used the thought of returning to help me work harder, dig deeper, and last longer. I stayed focused on what I wanted, and after a few weeks, it proved worth the effort.

Eventually, Don called me to say that there was some serious interest from a couple of teams. Edmonton was one, and I considered their offer. But then Don told me about the other team that was looking for some veteran help down the stretch. Even better, you could say the team and I had some history.

• • •

On January 14, 2000, I returned to the Toronto Maple Leafs for my third stint there. The last time I had played for the Leafs, our home had been Maple Leaf Gardens. But now they were playing at the Air Canada Centre, which had opened only a year earlier. Pat Quinn was at the helm of the Leafs at that time, as coach and general manager, and when I walked into the dressing room, it was a much different team than the one I had left just a couple of years earlier. Mats Sundin was still the big dog on the team, and Curtis Joseph was a star in net. They were a good hockey team, through and through, and unlike at the start of my career, I was coming back as just a small cog in a much bigger machine.

When I first got back to the city, Pat Quinn invited me to his condo for a meeting. He knew that if we met at the arena, the media frenzy would get out of hand and there'd be wild speculation. Pat was a talented, straight-shooting coach, and he didn't want those distractions. He wanted to hear from the horse's mouth what my expectations were. He told me he couldn't promise me anything, and I said to him, "Pat, whatever you need, I'm here to help. I'm a piece of the puzzle—you decide what role I play." As a player, I always felt that the bigger my role, the better. But I knew it was Mats Sundin's team now. And I understood where Pat was coming from. The team's lineup was set, and I was coming in as an extra forward. The last thing he and the team needed was for me to return to Toronto, only to try to take over the dressing room, causing shit and upsetting people as I tried to rekindle my glory days. But as far as I was concerned, the past was the past.

Each day, I waited patiently for the call from Pat, letting me know whether or not I'd be dressing that night. Sometimes I would have a couple of days' notice but other times, I wouldn't know until the morning of a game. At one point, I'd been out of the lineup for a few games in a row. We had just played a road game and were flying to another, and Pat had already told Glenn Healy he was playing the next night. When we got to our second stop, I suggested to Cujo that we go out for a beer—he wasn't going to be starting the next night, and I figured I'd be out of the lineup again, too. As we left the hotel, the entire coaching staff was in the lobby and they watched us walk out. I didn't give it a second thought, but at the game-day skate the next morning, Pat came up to me and just said, "You're in." He and I were both laughing as he skated away, and I made sure I was ready to go that night.

Pat ended up dressing me for twenty of the Leafs' final thirty-seven regular-season games, and I savoured every one of them. I watched Sundin's brilliance on the ice, Cujo's mastery in net, and Pat's smarts behind the bench, and I was proud to be a part of the success we were having. We won our division and earned the third seed in the conference playoffs that year. I was getting my wish of making another run for the Cup.

Our first playoff series was against the Ottawa Senators, and I dressed for two of the six games. The number of games I played didn't bother me. I wanted to see us win, and I would do whatever it took to help us get there, even if it meant having to watch from the press box. I was still undergoing my daily two hours of rehab throughout the playoffs. Given how much time I needed to get ready for a game, I wanted to play it safe by planning for the best-case scenario, making sure I would be ready to go if the call came. My diligence seemed to be paying off, too. Although I'd started the playoffs as a fill-in, in the first game of our next series, I was on the ice to face off against the New Jersey Devils.

The atmosphere was incredible that night. The ACC was packed and the game went back and forth all night. Dmitri Yushkevich put us up 1–0 early into the second period, but the Devils came right back and tied it up only a few minutes later. The rest of the period was scoreless, and then, just a few minutes into the third period, we struck again. Darcy Tucker, a teammate in Tampa Bay, was back in our corner, and he flipped the puck out of our zone. The puck rolled and bounced down the left wing, and I went chasing after it. Ken Daneyko, a veteran defenceman for the Devils, was right there with me—I could hear him right behind me as we raced for the puck, but I beat him to it and picked it up as it deflected off the boards and into the Devils zone. Ken positioned himself between me and the net, so I threw on the brakes and circled back up towards the blue line. Devils forward Randy McKay was coming back into the zone, and as he closed in on me, I pulled the puck away from him and flipped it towards the net. Tucker had come speeding up from behind the play, and he as he split the Devils defencemen, one of them—Eric Bertrand—knocked the puck down, right into Tucker's path. I started to skate towards the net, but there was no need. Tucker got a shot off on his backhand, and then buried the rebound past Martin Brodeur to give us a 2–1 lead.

The crowd exploded into cheers, and the energy never dropped for the rest of the game. We knew we had to keep the pressure on to come away with the win, so we kept throwing everything we could at Brodeur. A few minutes after Tucker's goal, I picked up the puck in our zone and started up the left wing. As I crossed our blue line, I cut through the centre of the ice. A couple of Devils tried to knock me off the puck, but I dodged their checks and muscled past them. I was off balance as I came across the New Jersey blue line, and as I looked up, I could see it was me and Tie Domi on a two-on-one. I had space, so I brought the puck back and unleashed a wrist shot on net. It beat Brodeur, but it didn't beat the goalpost. The fans all gasped as one as the puck pinged off the iron towards the boards, but the missed shot didn't bring their energy down one bit. When the whistle blew after the play, the crowd was still cheering and applauding. To my amazement, the crowd started calling out my name as the cheers just went on and on. It must have gone on for over a minute; I was completely overwhelmed. It was as though the fans knew I was done playing before I did!

We held on to the lead for the rest of the game and came out with a win. We tried to carry that momentum into the rest of the series, but we dropped the next two games to the Devils. We knew that everything was on the line in Game Four in New Jersey, because not that many teams can come back from a 3–1 deficit in a series. It was another close game, but Cujo was great and we managed to pull out a gutsy 3–2 win. I was sore going into the game, but I fought through it and ended up playing over thirteen minutes that night. I remember celebrating with Darcy Tucker on the ice after Tomas Kaberle scored the game winner. With less than two minutes to go in the third period, Scott Niedermayer had turned the puck over and Kaberle was able to beat Brodeur with a slapshot.

With the series even as we moved back to Toronto, it seemed like we were back on our feet and anything was possible. And that's exactly when the wheels came off the car for me.

We flew back home to Toronto after Game Four, and we had a couple days off before we hosted the Devils for the next match. The first morning after we got back, I woke up and found that my back was stiffer than usual. I tried to take it easy and ease out the stiffness. But later that day, I was carrying one of my young daughters, and as I tried to turn—*wham!*—my back shut down. That innocent act of turning as I held one of my kids was enough to throw my back out completely. I went to bed that night hoping it would feel better in the morning, but the next morning, I was still in agony. I could feel that this wasn't like the other times my back had acted up.

I wasn't willing to give up hope yet, so I went to work with Chris Broadhurst, hoping that would do the trick. But the hours of rehab I was doing each day just weren't getting the same results that they used to. It seemed my past had finally caught up to me, and I came to realize that it was going to take a lot of time and effort until my body recovered.

I wasn't able to play in Game Five, so I had to watch as the Devils beat us, 4–3, to take a 3–2 series lead. After the game, all the reporters wanted to know why I hadn't dressed. I told them the truth—that my back had seized up, I was getting a lot of treatment, and I hoped it would only last a couple of days. But another couple of days of rehab wasn't enough, and when Game Six rolled around, I had to sit and watch as we lost again to the Devils.

It was an ugly ending to the series—we only had six shots on goal all night. But we didn't lose to just another team; the Devils went on to win the Stanley Cup that year.

As I watched those last two games, it started to dawn on me that my career was over. I knew that I'd never again be able to play the way I wanted to for a full season, no matter how hard I tried. The grind had finally caught up to me, and after years of willing my body to cooperate, to respond to me, and to do more than it should, it had finally decided enough was enough.

● ● ●

I wasn't able to accept right away that my time in the NHL was done. I knew that I might still have been able to sign with a team, one that needed a cheap third-line winger or a veteran presence to train their younger players. But that wouldn't be a team that would be making a run to the Cup. I had to ask myself whether it was smarter to retire in Toronto, where everything had started for me, or sign elsewhere for one year on the chance that I just might get to play a few dozen more games.

I turned to Don Meehan for advice, and in his usual, plainspoken way, he told me that retiring was the smart thing to do. "It's your choice," he said, "but I can see the road to come." I knew that Don was talking to me as both my agent and my friend, and that he would leave the decision in my hands. We agreed on one thing—I had to make a decision before July 1, when players became free agents. And I knew I didn't want to sit around, uncertain and unsigned, until November. I was of the mindset that, whatever I decided to do, I would just go and do it.

Throughout my career, I had watched guys retire for lots of reasons. As I thought about the different ways the next year could play out, I thought about what it would be like for a player to retire injured versus one who's in great health when their career ends. When you retire injured, your decision is one of acceptance and compromise. For a player who is without injury, though, retirement can be challenging. We NHL players go a long time before anyone tells us that we're not good enough.

In some ways, it's easier to become an accountant than a professional athlete. As an accountant, if someone says that you're not good enough, you might get to rewrite a test as many times as you need until you prove to them that you are. But as a professional athlete, if someone says you're no good, you don't get another chance. When you hear for the first time that you're not good enough to play at the level you're used to, you'll do anything to try to prove those people wrong. One way or another, though, every player hears those words. If you're injured, at least you can blame your body or point to something external as the reason you can't play the same way anymore; the acceptance has already started, and, to a certain extent, you've seen it coming. I can't imagine what it would be like, if you're healthy, to have to realize all of a sudden that you're done.

As I thought about retiring, I tried to tell myself I was still young and strong. But I also had to admit to myself that bending over to tie my shoes had become difficult. I was confident that I could play thirty games, but I knew I wouldn't be able to play a full season anymore. It was a matter of my mind saying yes, but my body saying no, and I had to come to accept that, in this one area, my body was going to win.

So, on June 29, 2000, I officially retired from the NHL. The only person I spoke to before making the decision was Don Meehan. In private, I was at peace with my decision. But when I got to the news conference, all the nostalgia and doubt and gratitude that I'd been sitting on suddenly came through, and as I spoke to the reporters, I got choked up. Still, despite the heightened emotions, I felt good. I knew it was time. I was back in the city where my journey as a professional hockey player began.

Playing hockey the way I did, in the places I did, had made me who I was. I had broken into the NHL in Toronto as a teenager who was always ready to rough it up on the ice, and now, fifteen years later, I was leaving as a man with a wife and kids. For thirteen of those years, I had been in Toronto, and it was the only place where playing hockey had never felt like a job. If you were to take away any one of those steps in my career, or if I had done anything differently, I wouldn't be the same person. I had paid a price for the way I spent my years in the NHL. But now, after a decade and a half of setting records, endless hours of rehab, memorable wins and bitter losses, incredible teammates, and setbacks and successes, I was ready to face whatever came next.

11

Life After Hockey

rowing up on our farm, I had watched my parents pour money into the ground. Farming is a gamble every year when you plant your crops—you could put a lot of money into your farm in any given year and only get a little bit out of it. That's not a risk-reward equation that any stockbroker would take, but as a farmer, it's the only sort of life you know. For my parents, farming was what they knew and loved. My dad in particular couldn't and wouldn't turn away from it, no matter how much work it took. He embraced the challenges brought on by having to constantly react to every sort of issue, whether it was one he expected or one he never could have seen coming. Planning and preparation were key, and as the years went by, he learned from each mistake to make the next season just that much easier and more productive. For him, it was a lifelong process of give-and-take.

When I retired at thirty-three, I had a lot of years ahead of me.

As I was trying to find my way back into "real life," someone asked me if I had done any planning for my post-career life while I was playing. They were surprised when I responded that I hadn't given it any thought at all. Where my dad was always looking ahead to try to prepare for what might come next, I never felt that I could plan ahead while I played. So much of my time and energy were spent practising, training, staying healthy, and playing games. Sometimes I would think a little about what I would do when my career ended, but then the daily grind would take over again, and those thoughts would be pushed to the side; every resource I had was dedicated to playing the best hockey I could, and there wasn't much left over after that.

In my years in the NHL, I had picked up many life skills. I was experienced in leading a team through good times and bad. I knew how to manage and deal with people of every sort. I had an ability to focus that few people could match. But when it came to hard skills, I didn't have all that much to draw on.

My years in the NHL were characterized by one thing over and above everything else: attention. Every day, every shift, every movement took my complete concentration. To be able to play, I had to constantly pay attention to how my body was reacting, who I was lining up against that night, where my head was at. I also had to think about how my family was holding up, how my teammates were feeling, what the team needed, or where my career was headed. Nothing to do with hockey was too big or too small to be outside of my thoughts.

When my career ended, so many things changed. But that attention to the little things stayed with me. It takes focus to win a competition—whether it's on the ice or in the boardroom—and even if I was done with the NHL, I still wanted to be successful. I was disappointed that I wouldn't get to play hockey at the highest level ever again, but I wanted to achieve success in the next stage of my life, and to do that, I knew I couldn't just coast. I had to find a way to channel my energy and turn all the attention I'd been spending on hockey towards something new. I could accept that I wasn't a hockey player, and I knew that whatever I did next would never compare to my experiences in the NHL—what could be more fun than getting paid to play hockey in front of thousands of fans every night? So I would have to change my expectations. I didn't quite know where my next steps would take me, but I figured the best way for me to start was just by keeping myself busy and giving my full attention to whatever it was I was doing. I felt better about myself when I had a project, even more so when what I was doing was helping the people around me.

Being an ex-player is kind of like being a university student. You try your hand at a number of things to see what you're good at or what you might like, but you don't necessarily figure it out right away. You might change your mind a few times until you find the right place for you. After a while, I found my fit, the thing that would let me focus my energy. I bought a plot of land north of Toronto with a single goal in mind: I would build a new home. It sounded simple at first, but I quickly recognized that it was ambitious, to say the least. Still, I figured I wouldn't have time to sit around and feel sorry for myself if I was learning the basics of construction and building a house from the ground up.

It was slow going at first. I had some construction experience from my time on the farm as a kid, but a lot of years had passed since then, so there was a steep learning curve. I couldn't rely on my interest in the project to get me through, just as I couldn't become a car dealer simply because I loved cars. I had to actually be able to do the job well—the plan was for my family to live in the place, after all. So I hired a lot of skilled tradespeople to help me out. But I didn't want to just sit on the sidelines and let them do the work for me; I wanted to be in the thick of it with them, working side by side with the carpenters, welders, and landscapers to bring the project together. I still needed to be part of a team.

I found that the work cleared my head. The jobs were physical, and the days working on the site mirrored the days I might have spent back in the NHL. I'd wake up, take the kids to school, come home, and then spend a few hours of physical, interesting work that helped out the other guys on the crew—picking up and removing garbage, cleaning roads, general maintenance. It made the transition out of hockey a little easier, which I desperately needed.

I still had lingering problems from my career. I didn't sleep all the way through the night until eight months after I retired. Ever since my back had gone out, I would roll around in bed every night, unable to get comfortable. As my back seized up and flared, it would jolt me out of my sleep. I remember my first full night of sleep in retirement well—it was my first in ten years.

As our new home went up, I started to get a feel for the process. It didn't happen overnight. I was constantly adapting and learning, putting in the hours that it takes to learn any new skill. Eventually, I became so comfortable on the job site that friends started asking me to manage their home projects, too. Cujo asked me to oversee the construction of his new home and rink. Then Don Meehan did the same for his new house. I suddenly found myself busier on the construction front than I ever would have imagined. It looked like I was finally graduating to real life.

I also kept busy by making appearances at charity and corporate events. I got involved in some businesses and also worked as a community ambassador for the Leafs. So I didn't have a lot of time to dwell on the fact that I wasn't playing in the NHL anymore; I had more than enough to keep me busy on top of being a husband and a parent. And it wasn't like I was out of touch with the hockey world. Working as an ambassador for the Leafs was the best proof I could have had that Leafs fans are still the greatest hockey fans in the world, because they show up for everything, no matter what the event. They're always there, always supporting the Leafs, and they always will be.

• • •

Of course, the house I was building wasn't nearly as important as the people inside it, and I was lucky to have a beautiful family around me. When I was young and single, having a family was far from my thoughts. When I got up in the morning, I'd be thinking about hockey. I wouldn't have to worry about anyone other than myself, so I'd go to the rink and immerse myself in the game. I'd go home at the end of the night, and I'd be reviewing, celebrating, or dwelling on whatever I'd done on the ice that day.

That all changed when I met Denise. We met through Dave Ellett in the early 1990s. Dave had some friends visiting from Vancouver. He invited them all over for a party, and a few of us from the team showed up. I started talking with a young woman. Denise was with the group in from Vancouver, where she managed arbitration cases for the provincial government. She and I hit it off right away, and we never looked back. After Denise and I got married, Dave never let me forget that we had only met thanks to him. As we started our life together, I started to come out of my bubble, and when I learned that we'd be starting a family, my view of what was truly important started to change. But it wasn't until our first child, Kylie, was born, that everything really came into perspective.

It was 1996, and I was living in New York, playing for the Islanders. The NHL season was in full swing, but Denise was due any day, so I was on call—I wasn't going to miss the birth of our first child. When the call finally came, I raced to the hospital to be with her. We had been to birthing classes, bought all the baby gear, and done all the preparation that new parents do—we felt we were ready for whatever the evening would bring. We were so wrong.

There was a heavy snowstorm blowing in as I entered the hospital and found Denise. The snow kept falling over the next few hours until, finally, Kylie entered the world. But instead of the usual congratulations from the doctors and nurses that are supposed to follow the birth of a child, we heard urgent calls and a flurry of noise and movement.

There had been complications with the delivery, and doctors had discovered that the umbilical cord was wrapped around Kylie's neck. Because of that, no blood had been flowing to her body. When she was born, Kylie was white as a sheet.

The medical team leapt into action around us. The doctor inserted a needle and tube into Denise's arm to take blood for Kylie. He then collected the blood into a clean syringe and inserted the needle directly into Kylie's heart. The moments after that felt like a lifetime. They don't prepare you for episodes like that in birthing classes. It was the most anxious and terrifying experience of my life. Incredibly, after some time, Kylie began to stir as the blood circulated through her body, and the doctors were able to stabilize her.

But Kylie didn't have the same blood type as Denise. The doctors had had to take immediate action without any hesitation, and it saved Kylie's life, but because the wrong blood type had entered Kylie's body, she ended up in the incubator with jaundice. When it was clear that the worst had passed, the doctors were able to get Kylie on the proper blood type, and it looked like everything would be all right. As Kylie and Denise lay recovering in the hospital room, I was nearly shaking from the nerves. I knew that nothing on the ice would ever scare me as much as what I'd experienced in that hospital room. As much as I loved hockey, from that point on, I knew I'd never see the game the same way again.

That feeling only intensified after our other children, Kassie and Kody, were born. Fortunately, their births were not as eventful. Kassie, our second daughter, was born in 1997 in Toronto at Women's College Hospital, and Kody, our youngest, was born in 1999 in Chicago, while I was playing for the Blackhawks.

As our family grew, I felt my life becoming fuller and richer by the day. It was an experience unlike any I'd ever had. I had grown up as one of three boys, so having daughters was new to me. As a kid, if my dad said something to me, the answer was either yes or no. I wasn't used to the dynamics of having both daughters and a son. Our home never lacked for energy, that's for sure.

It was Denise's idea to give all three of our kids names starting with *K*. When she first proposed the idea, I said, "We aren't baseball players, so why the K?" Denise simply replied that she liked the names, and so that was that. I feel confident saying that I wear the pants in the family—Denise just tells me which pair to put on, and I'm happy to go with her advice.

Ever since she was young, Kassie was your typical middle child, and she was a very good athlete. Whatever sport she chose to play, Kassie was good at it, from volleyball to track and field. While Kody has seen most of my hockey highlights on YouTube and asked me about certain plays and moments, my girls have never asked me much about my playing days. They have heard more about what I did in the NHL from their friends and their friends' parents, and that's enough for them. To the girls, I'm just Dad. I drive them around and support them, and nothing could make me happier.

When I left hockey, I left behind a part of my life that I loved. But that wasn't necessarily a bad thing, because it meant I had more time in my life for the other things I cared about. My family had always been the best part of my life, and retiring just gave me an excuse to spend even more time with them. After I dropped the kids off at school in the morning, I would get working on our new house, and as the place took shape, I started to wonder what else I could create for my kids.

When I grew up, I knew everything within a five-mile radius of our farm. I was familiar with every tree on the land, every floorboard of our house, every tire tread on our machines. But outside of that, I knew next to nothing. My kids seemed to know what was going on halfway around the world, but they couldn't tell you what the end of our acreage looked like.

So, as part of my design for the house, I decided to build a barn on the property. This wouldn't be a barn for livestock or produce, though. No, this building was going to protect something even more important: an ice rink. I'd thought about putting in a pool, but we lived in Ontario, and I figured that I could use a rink six months out of the year, but there was no way I would get that much use out of a pool. I saw the rink as a way of sharing some of my childhood with my kids.

Although I wasn't planning to fill the barn with hay or animals, in a sense I was still farming in it. I was working with my hands, producing ice, tending to it, watering it, and keeping it in as perfect a condition as I could. I'd be driving equipment around the property in the pitch black of night, the headlights of my vehicle cutting through the dark in the same way the lights on the tractor would illuminate the fields when I was a kid.

Come late fall, I would be in the barn all evening, flooding and touching it up for hours. The kids would be helping me out, the hockey game would be on the TV, and the rink would slowly start to take shape beneath our feet. I was as happy as could be. As I scraped along the boards, smoothing out the corners, I thought back to my time as a rink rat in my dad's arena in Kelvington and how things seemed to have come full circle. The rink was my cathedral. It was my happy place where I could find a sort of peace and quiet that just didn't exist for me anywhere else.

After I'd finished tending to the ice and putting the kids to sleep, I'd often grab a stick and some pucks and just stand there in my boots, shooting pucks late into the night, just as I'd done as a kid. Other times, I would climb onto the Zamboni, throw on the Leafs game, and crack a beer as I flooded the ice. In those few minutes, I was in my comfort zone, and I was happy that, in some small way, I'd found my way back to hockey, even if it was different from what I was used to.

But come daylight, the rink was the kids' zone. Instead of a basement and a pool table, our family had a barn and a rink, and from October to April, the kids were on the ice all the time. Each Halloween, we hosted a holiday party. The kids would go out trick-or-treating with their friends, and then they'd all make their way back to the rink and go skating in their costumes. I looked forward to it because it was like an annual kickoff party for the rink. Throughout the rest of the winter, our kids would invite their friends over, and then, before we knew it, their parents would be there, too. Everyone would be crammed into the barn, jumping on and off the ice, watching hockey games, and staying over until late. The place was always packed. It was the perfect gathering place. It wasn't like anyone could wreck anything; it was just a barn, after all. Our rink was such a popular hangout that we had the number for a local pizza place right on the wall and an account set up for the rink. Anyone could order anytime, and the pizza guy would bring it right to the barn door.

I didn't think I could ever be happier than I was on those nights in the barn, surrounded by family and friends. Just having my kids around me brought me so much joy. I loved the day-to-day routine that came with being a dad—school pickups and drop-offs, making meals, chaperoning parties. It was a refreshing change from my days of practices, games, and travel when I was a player. As a player, I didn't get as many chances to experience those everyday moments that you have when it's just you and your kids in the car or around the dinner table. You don't get to spend enough quality time with your kids when you're a player, so I was thrilled that I could finally get up in the morning to hang out with my kids and be a part of whatever they had going on.

For my son, Kody, that meant being a part of sports in some way, shape, or form. From a young age, Kody was a talented athlete. At six years old, he was playing hockey in the winter and baseball in the summer. Baseball eventually dropped off his radar. As a young kid, Kody wanted to be where the action was, so when it was his turn to play in the outfield, he'd just sit down and play in the sand instead. Hockey was more Kody's game, and I was proud to see that. I wanted to be involved in that part of his life, but I also knew that I had to be careful not to let my past overshadow his time.

At first, I was happy to just watch Kody learn and develop as he rose through the ranks of the minor hockey system. Of course, I was excited to see what position he might choose to play. I had played defence as a kid because I thought it would be more fun—there were three lines of forwards and only four defenceman, so, in my mind, if I played defence, I would get more ice time. But I knew that lots of kids like the excitement of chasing the puck, and everyone learns the game differently, so I made sure I steered clear of making any decisions for Kody, and he ended up settling on right wing.

After a few years of watching Kody play, I started to help out with his teams, and eventually I ended up coaching some of them. If you want to find a way to connect to the game, then it all goes back to that simple question: Do you love it or do you just like it? If you love it, you'll find a way to stay involved. I thought that coaching might be my way of adapting to a new role in the game, and that it might be a nice excuse to get me out on the ice and try to pass on some of the skills and tips I'd learned in my career. I figured it would be fun and casual. Boy, was I wrong.

It wasn't the kids who made things difficult. It made me proud to see a group of kids I was coaching on the ice, learning to love the game of hockey and enjoying themselves along the way. But when we got off the ice, things took on a different tone, because the parents would swoop in. Ninety-eight percent of the parents I dealt with were awesome. It was the other 2 percent that made things difficult.

When I coached, one of my rules was that we wouldn't pay attention to stats. The important thing was for the kids to learn new skills and have fun, not keep a detailed account of their performance. On some occasions, there would be a parent who would come up to me, pointing at a game sheet and saying something like, "My son should have had an assist here." One time, I had a parent of a ten-year-old child come up and ask me why their son wasn't on the ice to take a faceoff in the last minute of a game. They handed me a sheet full of faceoff stats for every kid on our team, pointing out to me that their kid had the best percentage. I was stunned.

Some parents had a number for everything, but they didn't see the stats in the right way; they missed the parts of the game that were actually important. I watched every game, and I could tell who had had a good game and who hadn't. One boy might have played really well—great positioning, smart plays, enthusiastic teamwork— but not have anything to show for it on the score sheet, while another kid might have played sloppily but been in the right place at the right time to score a goal or two. The way I saw it, if you were on the ice or behind the bench, you were "inside the glass," and anybody inside the glass was a part of the game. Anybody outside the glass, on the other hand, was just a fan.

Not every parent was difficult to deal with, but with the ones who were, I never minced my words. Parents would often tell me they wanted their kid to play centre. They were convinced that centre was the best position—their child would take faceoffs, be where the puck was, and have a part in everything happening on the ice. It was the position for the best all-around players, in their eyes. Which is why they were always surprised when I responded, "Actually, the centreman is, in some ways, the least challenging position to play." After all, the defencemen and wingers had to learn to play without the puck, and they had to stick to their positions. That took discipline and intelligence. But a nine-year-old centreman just chased the puck around the ice. So, rather than just make a kid a centreman because their parents wanted them there, I tried to make sure that every kid learned how to really think and feel the game from every different angle and position.

As I coached the kids and dealt with the parents, my goal was simple: I wanted to make it easy for new players to love hockey. The world of hockey had come a long way since I first started playing. Back then, it was exclusively a winter sport. You played hockey in the winter, and then you switched to baseball or farming in the hot months. But when Kody started playing, hockey had become a twelve-month-a-year sport.

I see the 1972 Summit Series as the turning point. Before that, most professional hockey players came from three provinces— Saskatchewan, Ontario, and Quebec—and they grew up also playing sports other than hockey. But when we first saw the players who came from Europe, especially those who were in the army and who trained daily, things started to change. The exercise regimens got more intense. Youth started to focus exclusively on hockey at younger and younger ages. More and more money started to flow into professional hockey as it opened up outside of America. And, in just a couple of decades, we had players coming from dozens of countries around the world.

Anytime there was a chance for the team to travel to a tournament, parents would enthusiastically support it. They jumped at the chance to travel as far away as places like Colorado or Texas. There's something to be said for that sort of international experience, but sometimes, with so many people playing hockey around the world, you forget that you don't have to travel halfway across the continent to find a team that's just as good as yours. And really, for a kid, what's the difference between a hockey game followed by pizza and ministicks at a hotel in Chicago versus one in Kitchener?

Given how intense hockey could become for some kids before they even started thinking about making it big in the NHL, I wanted them to think about how they felt about the game in its most stress-free, fun form. If you're coaching kids, you're not just thinking about only one child, and you're not just thinking about your own son or daughter. Every decision you make throughout the year has to be made with all eighteen kids on the team in mind. Because you're not just training them for whatever sport they're playing. You're trying to teach them life skills—how to cooperate, how to accept success and failure graciously, how to focus on the job you're given. At the end of the day, it's just a game, and more than anything else, I wanted to pass along my love for it to a new generation who would carry that on.

Conclusion

The transition from being an athlete to finding a new normal for your everyday life isn't always easy. No matter how long I'm retired, I will never lose my drive to lace up the skates again and step out on the ice, just to feel that familiar rush one more time. A lot of athletes don't get a chance to return to the places and people that gave them that opportunity. I was fortunate enough to have that on the night that a banner with my number was raised at the Air Canada Centre.

The entire night was an emotional blur. When I first arrived at the arena, I was relaxed as I greeted the staff and friends I'd known for years and walked through hallways I'd been in hundreds of times before. I had been back to the ACC a number of times since I'd retired, but as I made my way down towards the rink, I started to get more restless with each step. It was a Saturday night in November, and as I made my way out to the bench where I'd spent so much of my life, I thought back to how many times I'd made that same walk over the years. I was in familiar territory, but I was used to approaching the rink in a hockey jersey, not a suit. I could hear the crowd rumbling above me, and even though I wasn't playing that night, I felt a familiar thrill jolt up my spine.

As the teams lined up at centre ice and the lights dimmed, all those thoughts were pushed out of my head. Andy Frost's voice came over the public address system, and a spotlight shone down on me. The noise from the crowd started to build steadily throughout Andy's introduction, but I kept staring at the ice. I knew that if I didn't focus on something specific, I was likely going to break down. I don't know if I could have held myself together if I hadn't had my family standing beside me. As the music was keyed up and the retrospective video played on the big screen, the crowd got louder and louder. For a moment, I let go of where I was and stepped back into the memories on the screen. I grinned at my many haircuts, thrilled at each goal, felt my fists clench at each fight, and smiled as each familiar face—guys I'd played with and competed against over the years—passed by on the screen.

The video ended, and as I walked out to the podium, the roars of the crowd were deafening. I'd never heard anything like it in my playing career; I could feel my chest rumbling with the noise. It was nearly a minute before the noise died down enough for me to get a word in. I barely remember the speech I made, but as I spoke, I could feel the history of the team and the pride of the fans in every moment. As the banner was raised, I looked up and thought of my parents watching from the box in the upper deck. It is hard to put into words what it means to experience a night like that one, but I can say this: seeing that banner raised was the greatest honour of my life.

Even with all the excitement around the banner raising, it actually wasn't the most memorable part of that day for me. That came earlier, as I was heading to the arena with my dad. My parents had come into town to watch the event, and as we made our way to the Air Canada Centre that night, my dad and I were talking about the other banners that already hung from the rafters. Icons like Darryl Sittler, Dave Keon, and Frank Mahovlich were memorialized there, and I still couldn't believe that my name would be among theirs. I was trying to explain how much all of that team history meant to me when my dad turned to me and said, "You know, the Leafs have always been my favourite team."

I was floored. My parents had both followed my career, but I never knew whether they cheered for a team because I was on it or because they actually cared about the team itself. My dad had never let on that he had a favourite team of any sort. Turns out he had loved the Leafs and the Yankees all his life; he'd just never got around to telling us.

"A fine time to tell me now!" was all I could say back. There I was, forty-two years old, and I was still learning something new about my parents.

That moment became all the more important to me because that night was one of the last ones I had with my dad. Two months after the banner ceremony, my parents were down in the Bahamas for a vacation. It was a well-deserved break for both of them—they'd just recently rented out the farm and moved to my grandparents' house in Kelvington, and it looked like they might be starting to slow down a bit and take some time for themselves. While they were on holiday, though, my dad came down with a bug of some sort. It looked like he had the flu, and one day, he decided to lie down and have a nap to rest. He never woke up. We discovered that my dad had indeed been sick—he'd had pneumonia, but he'd just been living and working through it. My dad didn't complain, so nobody had known how sick he was. The lingering effects of the sickness had caused what the doctors called a silent heart attack.

When Dad passed away peacefully in his sleep, we were devastated. I went from a period of such joy and pride to one of immense, overwhelming sadness. But I was inspired by my mom's strength, and as time passed, I saw how much I still had to be grateful for. One of our last shared experiences as a family—my parents, Denise, my kids—was that ceremony, and it made it all the more special. My three kids are the best part of my life, and after I lost my dad, I started to reflect more on my own role as a father.

I've always felt that it's not what you do that matters, it's why you do it. What good is success on the ice if you don't have anyone to share it with? I didn't just like hockey, I loved it. And I was more than willing to do anything to keep playing, even when I was told to stop. I was never part of a team that won a Stanley Cup, but I still don't regret a single thing about my career. If I had never fought, maybe I would have been able to score twenty-five goals a year for fifteen years. But that's not a trade I would ever make, because if I changed anything in my past, I wouldn't have the life I do today.

All the endless hours of rehab, the thousands of acupuncture needles, and the sleepless nights and constant pain—it was all worth it. Not just because of my love for the game, but also because of my love for my family. I had lived and breathed hockey for as long as I could remember, and it had given me and my family a wonderful life. Now it was time to go live it.

A Tribute to My Dad

My family has always been close with each other. Recently, my mom and my brother Donn stumbled upon a poem that my mom wrote several years ago in tribute to my dad. She wrote it sometime after I retired from the NHL. Whenever I read it, it brings back all kinds of memories—memories of me playing hockey with my brothers, of Kelvington, and of how my mom and dad would do anything for their friends and family. It tells the story of one of my favourite moments from my teenage years.

When I was about to leave the Notre Dame Hounds to play in the WHL, my dad told me that if I played in Regina, I would get a new Oldsmobile. If I went on to play in Prince Albert, I would get a shiny new Volkswagen. But if I played in Saskatoon, I would end up having to drive the old brown 1972 Chevy pickup truck with the three-on-the-tree stick shift. Let's just say I ended up getting a lot of miles out of that truck.

My dad used to play senior hockey in the 1950s, and one of his biggest rivals was Daryl Lubiniecki, who went on to become the general manager of Saskatoon. My dad's nickname when he played was "Killer," but over time, things came full circle, and my dad grew to respect Daryl. By the time my dad called Lubie about giving one of my best friends, Kelly Chase, a shot at a tryout, he'd come to understand that the Saskatoon Blades were a great organization. From the owners on down, hockey was more than just a game to them.

My mom wrote this poem for all the kids from Kelvington who played the game, not just for those of us who made it. And when my mom talks about all the kids "plus one," that extra one is Kelly Chase. Because Kelly was always one of us.

This poem explains life in small-town Saskatchewan and all my ties to hockey. It's an ode to all our closest family and friends in the game—guys like Barry Melrose, Joey Kocur (and the rest of the Kocur family), and Dennis Beyak, because Dennis is as good a person as you will ever find.

I hope you enjoy it.

Thirty-five Years + Kelvington Kids + One
Dedicated to Les and Lubie

When Killer cracked the lineup of the then Wesley's,
Les, as he's better known today,
Crushed every opponent that got in his way.
It all started back in '53.

Suiting up later, like four score years and ten,
A brother, an uncle, plus one's family friend.
The talents of Murray, Sexsmith knew,
Undoubtedly the greatest of the Kelvington crew.

Along came son Donn and like father, like son,
His playing days ended with one leg on the bum.
Next came Wendel, and the battle was on.
Les and Lubie fought it out with Rick, Nate's son.
"If you go to Regina, you get the Olds,
If you go to PA, you get the shiny new Volks,
If you go to Saskatoon, it's the old brown truck!"
Came a whisper from the corner, "Aw, shucks."
In the darkness of his bedroom a tear rolled down his cheek,

For you see it was a Blade he really wanted to be.
A phone call from Dennis soon straightened things away,
"He respects you as a father," was all he had to say.
Now approaching Lubie at a Kelvington do,
Son Kerry firmly stated what he wanted to do.
"Year following Wendel might be pressure indeed."
Kerry boldly replied, "He's Wendel. I'm me!"

Then a call from the south proved action again,
"Plus One" was in trouble, and could you do something then?
"I'll talk to Lubie, Kelly, is all I can do."
For you see, "Plus" was a native son, too.

We drove and cheered, the Kocurs and us.
For Joey and Kory fit right in the rut.
Joe came first and Kory came next,
With toughness and talent they showed us their best.

Barry Melrose, a pupil, a cousin, a son,
Provided a rivalry, making things fun.
Opposing first as a player and then as a coach.
We eagerly awaited his next new approach.

There were moments of tension for all mothers and sons,
And many's the time we had to succumb,
But with Roger and Donna and Marcel we learned
Of values and traditions other clubs yearned.

Throughout thick and thin, Les and Lubie remained friends,
And for the love of the sport they might do it again!
For well Lubie knew how his business is run.
Knew Les wanted best for the native sons.

Written by Alma Clark

Acknowledgments

There are many people I would like to thank for making this book possible. I wouldn't even be in a position to write a book if it weren't for all the love and support I had growing up. So, thanks to my mom and dad and my two brothers, Donn and Kerry.

It all starts with my hometown of Kelvington, Saskatchewan. I owe a lot to the people in that great little town.

I also thank everyone involved with the Notre Dame Hounds in Wilcox, Saskatchewan. I had a lot of good times at Notre Dame and made some lifelong friends during my time there.

I can't say enough about the entire staff of the Saskatoon Blades. They treated me like gold, and I am forever grateful for that. Thanks also to my awesome billets in Saskatoon, Nettie and Ray Fenner.

Don Meehan is more than just my agent, he is my friend. So thanks to Don and all the staff at Newport Sports.

I can't say enough about Chris Broadhurst and all the endless hours he spent with me getting me ready to play hockey.

Thank you to everyone involved with the Toronto Maple Leafs. I am proud to say I started and ended my career with the Leafs.

I would like to thank all the teammates, staff, and fans of all the teams I played for over the course of my NHL career. There are far too many to mention them all but they all played a big role in my playing career.

In my post-hockey career, I would like to thank Andrew Jackson and everyone involved with Jackson Events.

I would like to thank the Maple Leafs alumni and all the other NHL alumni. I have been lucky enough to take part in some amazing alumni events all across Canada and meet some great people along the way.

Many thanks to Jim Lang for helping me to write this book and the countless hours of hockey talk.

Finally, I would like to thank my wife, Denise, and my three kids, Kylie, Kassie, and Kody.

—WENDEL CLARK

• • •

To say this book project came as a bit of surprise to me is a major understatement. In the spring of 2015, my agent, Brian Wood, called and asked me if I was interested in co-writing a book with Wendel Clark. It took all of a second to say yes. Then came the kicker: Simon & Schuster wanted the manuscript completed in just over seven months. Brian asked if I thought I could pull it off in that short a time.

Well, this is Wendel Clark we are talking about. So you're darn right I thought I could pull it off.

But completing a task like this in that amount of time required a lot of help. Fortunately, I had many people by my side who helped me all along the way.

First and foremost, I need to thank my lovely wife, Patricia, and our girls, Adriana and Cassandra. Without their patience and understanding of the hours needed to complete a project like this, the book never would have been written.

I'd like to thank my mom and dad for giving me the work ethic that helped me meet all the tight deadlines we had to meet along the way.

I've said it before and I will say it again, my agent Brian Wood is a pro and he really worked his tail off to help bring this deal together. Thanks, Brian—we are a good team!

The folks at Simon & Schuster Canada are first-class all the way. It all starts with publisher Kevin Hanson, who always leads from the front. A big stick tap to my trusted editor Brendan May for keeping everyone focused on the task at hand. Brendan, you're a good man.

I would like to thank the management and staff at the radio station I work at, 105.9 The Region, for being so understanding throughout the entire process.

I would also like to thank Andrew Jackson at Jackson Events. Andrew is one of Wendel's most trusted advisors, and he was the glue that helped make this deal happen.

I spoke to a number of people that provided invaluable insight and information that helped make this book what it is. They include former Maple Leafs trainer Brent Smith, former Maple Leafs media relations director Pat Park, and longtime hockey reporter Howard Berger. Thanks to hockey historian Paul Patskou for finding long-lost Wendel highlights once shown on CH-TV and Global Sportsline. Thanks to Sportsnet's John Shannon. And a big thanks to Benny Ercolani from the NHL's archives office for finding the original score sheet from the night Wendel scored his first NHL goal.

I'd like to thank some of Wendel's former teammates for taking the time to speak with me, in particular Wendel's closest friends, Dave Ellett (what a beauty) and the always entertaining Russ Courtnall (what a memory!).

I also had the pleasure of speaking with members of Wendel's family, including his wife, Denise, his son, Kody, his charming mother, Alma, and his older brother, Donn.

The

The

The

The

The

The

I would also like to thank Don Chesney, the Yorkton Terriers, and Barry Marianchuk.

A big shout-out goes to Don Meehan and everyone at Newport Sports.

Many thanks to the informative websites that were needed to tell Wendel's story. They include Saskatoonblades.com, NHL.com, Mapleleafs.com, Hockeydb.com, Hockey-reference.com, Hockeyfights.com, and YouTube.com.

And most of all, I would like to thank the man of the hour, Wendel Clark.

While we'd had a few previous meetings, this book was written between September 2015 and March 2016. During those months, I was fortunate to spend a lot of time with Wendel. We met well over a dozen times and had some fascinating conversations about hockey, life, family, and our shared love of hamburgers.

When friends and family found out I was working on a project with Wendel I was asked the same question numerous times: "What's he like?"

My answer was the same every time: "He's just Wendel."

With Wendel Clark, what you see is what you get. There is not a phony bone in the man's body. Which goes a long way to explaining his ongoing popularity with Leafs fans all across Canada who have had the pleasure of meeting him.

Many of our meetings took place at the Second Cup at Bay and Lakeshore (good cookies!) in Toronto, and I can honestly say that each conversation was more enjoyable and more informative than the one before.

A man can learn a lot by spending some time and talking to Wendel Clark, and I like to think I'm a better man for spending all that time with him writing this book.

—JIM LANG

VBKUAK 407GM 266 458.